It's rare to find a book so wise and helpful that I want to put it in the hands of every pastor, parent, and future leader I know. *The Spirit of Our Politics* is such a book. Michael Wear weaves together his expertise on American politics and Dallas Willard's vision for the centrality of discipleship in the Christian life. In doing so, he accomplishes the rare feat of merging political theology and spiritual formation in ways that are profoundly necessary yet virtually absent in the current political discourse both in the church and in broader society. This book opens a window, letting a new, hopeful breeze blow into the dark, airless room of American politics. *The Spirit of Our Politics* should be required reading for every Christian in America.

Tish Harrison Warren, author of *Liturgy of the Ordinary* and *Prayer in the Night*

I know many people I respect as spiritually mature. I know many people who know politics from the inside out. I don't know very many who fit both of those categories. Michael Wear does. This book shows a smart, bold, hopeful way forward, paying attention to what Dallas Willard would tell us is the *real* conspiracy—the inbreaking kingdom of God. If you have never thought spirituality and politics belong in the same sentence, this is the book you must read.

Russell Moore, editor-in-chief, *Christianity Today*

From the very first sentence, I knew this was the book I'd been waiting for. In *The Spirit of Our Politics*, Michael Wear not only diagnoses the root of the problem that has led us here but also offers a compelling way forward. This book is essential reading for anyone who takes seriously the commission of Jesus to go out and be the salt and light we are called to be.

Christine Caine, founder, A21 and Propel Women

The Spirit of Our Politics is the most urgently needed and clearly articulated discussion of faith and politics I have ever read. If a large number of people were to read and embody the moral and political knowledge available here, it would immeasurably enhance our country—not to mention the church.

> **John Ortberg,** founder, Become New; author, *If You Want to Walk on Water, You've Got to Get Out of the Boat*

The Spirit of Our Politics is one of the most important books of our time. In this brilliant text, Michael Wear draws on Dallas Willard's insights to argue that our personal character deeply influences our political landscape. While Wear delves into the complexities of how our politics reached its current state, this book isn't merely an analysis of the past; it radiates with a visionary outlook for the future. Instead of merely lamenting what has been, Wear offers a thoughtful and constructive path forward. Every reader, regardless of their political inclination, should take up the invitation contained in this essential reading. Through it, we are prompted to reflect, *What kind of person would I like to be—and how can my conclusion shape a better political tomorrow?*

> **Joshua DuBois,** CEO of Values Partnerships; former executive director, The White House Office of Faith-Based and Neighborhood Partnerships

Michael Wear has written an important book at an important time. The work of self-government is challenging when the world makes partisanship a religion. We might have important disagreements on public policy, but as brothers in Christ, Michael and I share the same calling—to glorify God and to enjoy him forever. As Christians work to build something more constructive, Michael gives us worthy reflections on a complicated topic.

> **Ben Sasse,** president, University of Florida; former US senator from Nebraska

The Spirit of Our Politics gets to the heart of our current divided politics. Michael Wear has written a powerful call that affirms the agency each citizen has to contribute to a healthier and more just politics and society. As a Christian, I found here an inspiring path to return to the heart of our faith and build a culture of engaged, faithful service. Our politics would be dramatically healthier if *The Spirit of Our Politics* was our guide, and I encourage my colleagues, and all readers who seek a positive future for our politics, to read it.

Chris Coons, US senator from Delaware

Most books we read force us to explore either society and culture or a personal interior journey. Both are good, but they really belong together. *The Spirit of Our Politics* gets right to the heart of what it takes to be effective, loving, and joyful in public life. It's the book I wish I had written myself as a practical, informed, realistic, visionary, and wise guide to spiritual formation for civic renewal in our generation.

James Catford, founding chair, the Center for Christianity and Public Life; literary advisor to the Dallas Willard Estate; ministry team member, Renovaré

Liberal democracy depends on virtuous citizens who are committed to its survival, yet it often fails to inculcate these virtues. Michael Wear outlines the role of Christianity in helping to lay the foundations for virtuous civic engagement in an era when the faith is arguably in jeopardy of becoming a victim of vituperative culture wars. Based on a sensitive reading of Scripture and deep experience working in contemporary politics, Wear offers a vision of Christian politics rooted in service and compassion, not conquest or domination. This is a crucial book for thinking about the future of American Christianity.

Elizabeth Bruenig, staff writer, *The Atlantic*

If you are exhausted by and exasperated with politics, this book is for you. *The Spirit of Our Politics* won't try to drum up your enthusiasm for our broken political system; it will draw your attention to a greater and truer story—and the way that story should then shape our common life together. Michael Wear has given us the gift of diagnosing the deeper spiritual problems underneath our divisions and disagreements—and proposing a better path forward.

Kaitlyn Schiess, author, *The Ballot and the Bible*

Michael Wear has clarified and focused our attention on the gaping divide between the beliefs that so many of us profess and the contemptuous politics that so many of us practice. People of faith have a long way to go to align the calling to love one another with the actions to create a politics grounded in that love. Wear offers countless selections from Scripture and scholars alike to help us in that urgent path of discipleship.

Tim Shriver, cofounder, Unite

A must-read for American Christians. Michael Wear leads us away from the intractable right-left disagreements and toward a far more important question: *How is American politics shaping us spiritually?* No matter where you are on the political spectrum, this book will help you move away from being discipled by your political party and toward being discipled by Jesus.

Justin Whitmel Earley, business lawyer; author, *The Common Rule, Habits of the Household,* and *Made for People*

Michael Wear is a trusted voice to a generation of Christ followers looking to express their faith in every area of culture, including politics. *The Spirit of Our Politics* is the book that is needed today, to help us to separate what needs to be separate and integrate that which will make us whole—individually and as a nation.

Annie F. Downs, New York Times bestselling author, *That Sounds Fun*

Michael Wear is a man of deep faith who clearly brought his love for Jesus to his work in the White House. His book *Reclaiming Hope* offers important insight about his time working in the public square for the legitimate and necessary place of both faith and people of faith in today's political environment, and it deserves serious attention.

His Eminence Timothy Cardina Dolan

Reclaiming Hope is an important and extremely timely book. It is partly a memoir, partly a reflection on the relationships between faith and governing power, and partly a road map for navigating the unprecedented social and cultural changes we are facing. It's readable and thought-provoking. Get it, read it, and talk to others about it.

Timothy Keller, author, *The Reason for God* and
The Prodigal God

In *Reclaiming Hope*, Michael Wear makes a powerfully compelling case for engaging the intersection of politics and religion. Drawing from his personal and singular experience in the White House under the Obama administration, Wear writes a lifeline for these times—that despite any personal differences, hope can unite. The pages in your hand could give you hope and lead and guide us forward as a nation. We can all reclaim hope and carry it with us.

Ann Voskamp, New York Times bestselling author,
One Thousand Gifts and *The Broken Way*

The

SPIRIT
OF OUR
POLITICS

Spiritual Formation and the
Renovation of Public Life

MICHAEL WEAR

ZONDERVAN
BOOKS

ZONDERVAN BOOKS

The Spirit of Our Politics
Copyright © 2023 by Michael Wear

Published in Grand Rapids, Michigan, by Zondervan. Zondervan is a registered trademark of The Zondervan Corporation, L.L.C., a wholly owned subsidiary of HarperCollins Christian Publishing, Inc.

Requests for information should be addressed to customercare@harpercollins.com.

Zondervan titles may be purchased in bulk for educational, business, fundraising, or sales promotional use. For information, please email SpecialMarkets@Zondervan.com.

ISBN 978-0-310-36719-2 (softcover)
ISBN 978-0-310-36723-9 (audio)
ISBN 978-0-310-36722-2 (ebook)

Cover design: Curt Diepenhorst
Cover illustration: Olga Moonlight / Shutterstock
Interior design: Kait Lamphere

Printed in the United States of America

23 24 25 26 27 LBC 5 4 3 2 1

To Saoirse and Ilaria—
with your father's unyielding love
for who you are
and great hope
for the kind of people you are becoming.

It is a serious thing to live in a society of possible gods and goddesses, to remember that the dullest and most uninteresting person you talk to may one day be a creature which, if you saw it now, you would be strongly tempted to worship, or else a horror and a corruption such as you now meet, if at all, only in a nightmare. All day long we are, in some degree, helping each other to one or other of these destinations. It is in the light of these overwhelming possibilities, it is with the awe and the circumspection proper to them, that we should conduct all our dealings with one another, all friendships, all loves, all play, all politics.

C. S. Lewis, *The Weight of Glory*

CONTENTS

INTRODUCTION

Our politics is sick.

Few would take issue with that assessment, but the problem goes deeper than most of us realize or admit. Politicians blame the "other side" for the problems in our politics. We are told that total victory is on the other side of our opponents' defeat, and that if we could only marginalize or eliminate certain kinds of people or forces, our politics would be made well. We tell ourselves that our political sickness is the result of structures over which we have no control and corrupt politicians we never supported. The siren song calls out to us: *You are what is right with America. You made America. You need to take America back from them.* This is the spirit of politics today, but we cannot place all of the blame on "them."

Our politics is suffering not from appendicitis but from leukemia. The problem is not that something has gone wrong, but that the very logic on which the entire system operates exacerbates the sickness. We don't need an appendectomy; we need new marrow in our bones.

This diagnosis isn't what we expect in discussions of political reform, nor is it what is regularly offered. For those who are frustrated enough by our politics to think change is necessary (most

Americans!) *and* who are motivated enough to do something about it (a minority of Americans!), our political system easily offers enemies to be blamed and structural changes to pursue. This is not entirely off the mark. A healthier politics would be supported by, and produce, structural reforms and the diminished influence of bad actors. But something more significant is at play: our politics is the way it is because it reflects the desires and allowances of voters.

In October 2020, as the presidential campaign came to its conclusion, fifteen of the most respected social scientists in the world came together to issue a dire warning about American politics and a phenomenon they called "political sectarianism," defined as "a poisonous cocktail of othering, aversion and moralization [that] poses a threat to democracy."[1] We will discuss this phenomenon at greater length, but for now it's enough to say that this "poisonous cocktail" has spilled beyond the confines of those most directly engaged in the political process and into most other areas of life. The American Psychological Association found that 52 percent of Americans felt additional stress due to the 2016 election—they called it "election stress disorder"—and recommended steps people could take for relief.[2] Teachers reported students were fearful about the election outcome, even to the extent that they were having nightmares about it.[3]

I know of churches where people who had served in leadership together for years were no longer able to even attend the same church because of political animosity. There are church small groups that met for decades that have broken up because they could not get through a Bible study without breaking out into rancorous political dispute. There are parents and children who are estranged from each other over political disagreements.

Our political disrepair is not limited to political sectarianism, of course. However, political sectarianism touches and exacerbates other political problems, such as distrust in government, legislative inaction, and the growth of extra-legislative policymaking through the executive and judicial branches, a rise in political violence, an array of injustices that our politics leaves unaddressed, and the antagonisms and harms our political system promotes.

Where is the Christian in all of this? The problem is not so much that there are broad swaths of committed Christians who make exceptionally bad contributions to our politics, but rather that there is nothing exceptional about their politics at all. We are so often driven by the same self-interested, self-protecting motives as other voters. We are so often prone to the same partisan rationalizations, the same politics of contempt, as our political opponents, whoever they are. Instead of being a positive, countercultural force in our politics, Christians have too often been a part of the problem—not *because* of what our faith requires but *in spite of* it. And the public suffers because of this failure.

For nearly a decade now, conversations about faith and politics have been dominated by Donald Trump and the evangelical response to him. However, our political dysfunction did not begin with Donald Trump, although his rise caused many to reevaluate their own approach to politics. Many Christians now embrace the identifier of "politically homeless." This is an improvement over a view that Christians must necessarily belong to any particular party as a matter of faithfulness, but it misses the point. It suggests a nostalgia for a time in the past when, supposedly, it was obvious which political party deserved the support of all Christians. *We must understand that the crisis today is not that Christians are now politically homeless, but rather that they ever thought they could make their home in politics at all.*

There is no single proposition by which our politics will be set right or by which Christians can easily align themselves on "the right side." Instead, we must ask, *What kind of person would I like to be? What kind of politics would I like to contribute to building?* This book is not primarily about describing what is wrong with our politics, though that will be necessary. We must turn to what we will do, what we can build, and who we will become.

A BREAKING POINT. AN OPPORTUNITY

The stakes are high. They include the future of the political life of our nation and extend to the well-being of the church in America and the ripples we send out to the global church. The stakes include our own souls, and the souls of those we influence, as we come to understand that what happens in our political life is not somehow quarantined from other aspects of our lives.

A few years ago, I received a call from a friend who was a pivotal leader in mobilizing voters in support of Donald Trump's candidacy and of conservative Republicans generally. We have worked on areas of common concern before, and I assumed my friend was reaching out on one of those issues. Instead, my friend said this:

> Michael, I know this is a little out of the blue, but I was hoping you might find the time to meet with my daughter. She's been deeply troubled by what's happening in our politics, and while I've tried to explain it, she doesn't understand my position on Trump. She's no longer attending church, and she's struggling in her faith. I want her to meet with a faithful Christian who

just has a different approach to politics than I do. Michael, to be honest, I no longer care all that much about the future of my daughter's politics. I just want her to start going to church with her family again.

Oddly, perhaps, this conversation was one of the most hopeful I've had in recent years. Here was someone who had invested their professional life in political advocacy, but who nonetheless was willing to set aside their politics out of love for their daughter. How many of us would do the same? How many of us would say we'd prefer to lose in our political ambitions if it meant others might draw closer to Jesus? How many of us would say we'd prefer to sacrifice political advantage if it meant *we* might draw closer to Jesus?

I made a decision early in my life that I wanted this to be my posture. I became a Christian when I was fifteen years old after reading the book of Romans in the Bible. When I went to church the next Sunday and the pastor asked everyone to close their eyes and bow their heads while he offered an opportunity to pray the sinner's prayer, I raised my hand. *That's it*, I thought. *I'm a Christian.* And I was.

Pretty soon, though, I had questions about what becoming a Christian meant for my life, the one I was living now, day by day. What did it mean to hand it all to Jesus, and how might I go about doing that? Answering these questions has been the pursuit of my life. It is the work and example of Dallas Willard, more than that of any other writer or thinker, that has been most helpful to me in this pursuit.

Dallas was born on September 4, 1935, in the middle of the Great Depression. He was raised for much of his life on a farm just outside of Buffalo, Missouri. His childhood was one of true poverty and was marred by tragedy, including the death of his mother when he was just a toddler. Dallas would find loving relationships with adults as a child, especially with his older sister and her husband, but he felt a profound sense of estrangement and isolation as a child, which influences his writing and theology. The circumstances of Dallas's life left him uninterested in a faith of empty slogans and feckless promises.[4] He was after reality.

Dallas attended Tennessee Temple University, received an MA from Baylor University, and graduated with a PhD in philosophy from the University of Wisconsin. He was hired to join the faculty of the University of Southern California's philosophy department, which would serve as his academic home for nearly fifty years. There he was, a Christian man from a humble background, now ensconced among a largely secular elite—operating within the world of academic philosophy, with its own rules and measures of success and status—while also teaching in churches and writing books about life with Jesus. All of this would come to mean a great deal to me.

When I was working in the White House, someone sent me a copy of Willard's book *The Divine Conspiracy*, which served as a revelation, in many ways launching a second spiritual awakening in my life. I was not raised in a family of committed Christians. I was not quite sure what to do with this life I had given to Jesus. What did it mean to follow him? Is the pinnacle of the Christian life really raising your hand in an auditorium? Was the most exhilarating and engaged part of the Christian's life really meant to be the process of deciding to be one?

Dallas offers a clear answer: *No. Life is, most crucially, about the kind of person we are and the kind of person we are becoming.* Eternal life, the kind of life Jesus offers, is "the Kingdom Walk, where, in seamless unity, we 'Do justice, love kindness, and walk carefully with our God' (Micah 6:8). We learn to walk this way through apprenticeship to Jesus."[5] That is, life with Jesus is about all of life, not just what we do at church, but *all* of life.

I had thought this was what I had been reading in my Bible, and I had heard rumors of it in church, but Dallas gave me confidence that such a vision was real and could be trusted. *The Christian life is not about a moment, but rather about a life. The resources that are available through Jesus are actually up to the task of meeting our real, lived existence.* I have come to believe that the kinds of ideas Dallas Willard taught about Jesus and the life he offers have the power to reorient our politics for the good of the public.

The problem, the fatal error, is that our culture, our churches, and many, many individuals—Christians and others—have a view of a domesticated, personalized, and privatized Jesus who is simply not up to the task of our greatest public challenges. We, as individuals and as a culture, often do not trust that Christianity has credible resources that are valuable for our public and political lives. We take great pride in our doctrinal acumen, our "high view" of this or that, while we act as practical atheists in our public life.

It would be not only insufficient but also inaccurate for Christians to blame outside forces—secularism, liberalism, political correctness, an antagonistic popular culture, etc.—for this development. Rather, this privatized, domesticated view developed in America with both the explicit and tacit contributions of Christians.

These are the two primary modes in which Christianity is regularly considered in our political life: it is either dismissed as irrelevant or co-opted into a tool for advancing one policy or another. *When it comes to politics today, Christianity is viewed either as useless or as something to be used.*

This is not just a problem for our politics, which is deprived of resources it desperately needs; it poses a crisis for the church. If Christianity is about whole-life discipleship to Jesus Christ, and it is, then the view that the way of Jesus is not up to the task of our politics makes that discipleship impossible.

But politics has much to do with discipleship because the kind of person we are when dealing with public things—taking political action, talking about political or cultural issues—is not removed from the kind of person we are in "real life."

As you read this book, I want you to keep in mind the stakes the consequence and costs of continuing on our current path:

1. The public, and our politics, will continue to suffer from a lack of Christian resources. Our social relations will be strained and regularly fracture.
2. Christians' own formation into Christlikeness will continue to be undermined by their own lack of confidence that the way of Jesus holds up in politics and public life, a lack of confidence that cannot help but infect the whole life of the person.
3. This lack of confidence, displayed in public, leads Christians to doubt the very reality of their faith and leads non-Christians to never consider whether the faith testifies to reality at all.

We have fundamentally misunderstood the nature and possibilities of Christian influence in our politics. We need a paradigm shift in the way we think about that influence. After you've read this book, my hope is that you will find that you now have a new language for talking and thinking about politics that is not detached from the rest of your life. I hope you will gain a new vision that makes sense of politics as an aspect of your whole life—the life you are living with, by, and for God.

In the first chapter, I set the table with some context regarding the state of our politics, with particular attention to the previously mentioned concept of "political sectarianism."

In the three chapters that follow, I provide an overview of the philosophical shift that led to the detachment of religious knowledge—and, therefore, spiritual formation—from public life, which Willard referred to as the "disappearance of moral knowledge." Then I discuss how truncated views of the gospel— what I call a "fixer gospel" and a "toolbox gospel," and what Willard called "gospels of sin management"—are directly related to a flawed Christian approach to politics and public life. Then I discuss Willard's conception of kingdom living and how it applies to our approach to politics. These chapters reorient our relationship to politics, placing it squarely under a view of our life in the kingdom of God.

In chapter 5, I argue that gentleness ought to characterize Christians' public witness. In chapter 6, I share Dallas Willard's model for spiritual formation—VIM (vision, intention, means)— and offer it as a way of constructing, guiding, and carrying out our role as citizens, out of the conviction that spiritual formation is central to civic renewal. Chapter 7 then offers spiritual disciplines, some old and some new, that will help us become the kind of people who will contribute to the kind of politics we hope for.

Chapter 8 is written with two specific groups in mind— pastors and parents. Instead of casting greater burdens on pastors, I offer encouragement to keep first things first and prioritize the shepherding of the congregation, including an attentiveness to the social and political that is not merely derivative of modern political culture. Pastors are to be teachers of the nations, and they ought to have much to contribute to our civic life. Unfortunately, in part due to politics, many clergy now feel disempowered and flat-footed. This must change for the health of our churches and the well-being of our communities.

Parents, of course, play a central role in the spiritual formation of their children, and I argue that politics can provide opportunities for formation in family life instead of just stoking familial conflict.

Finally, chapter 9 casts a vision for how a changed people can transform our politics.

I, too, am skeptical of a self-interested, tribalistic, and antagonistic Christian influence in politics that calls itself Christian but looks, sounds, and acts nothing like Christ. I am writing this book because of my great disappointment with the way many Christians conduct themselves in public and because of my great hope for the possibilities should more people choose to become the kind of people our politics needs.

I would like to gain a fresh hearing for Jesus in our public life for the good of the public.

Chapter 1

OUR POLITICAL SICKNESS

We cannot separate out the kind of politics we have—our laws, our political leaders and institutions, our political culture—from the kind of people we are. Our politics is doing great harm, materially and spiritually, and if that is to change, it is vital that we recognize the ways in which our politics is *ours*. If we were a different kind of people, our politics would be different.

Politics affects the material circumstances of our lives. This alone is justification for Christians to care about politics and to take up the responsibility to participate in the political process. What is becoming more apparent—though it was always the case—is that our politics shapes us spiritually. Our political culture, along with our thoughts, feelings, and actions related to politics, affects who we are as people.

This book and much of your life and the lives of those around you in your family, your church, and your community will not make sense to you unless you understand that politics has a great deal to do with the kind of people we are. You do not have a "political self" that is separate and distinct from the

1

"real you." You are just you. Thoughts, feeling, and actions that are characteristic for a person when they are dealing with politics are not quarantined off from the rest of the person. If you are the kind of person who lies during political arguments to get your way, you are the kind of person who lies during political arguments to get your way. If you are the kind of person who wishes ill to fall on those you disagree with politically, you are that kind of person.

We will return to this idea later in this book, but the point to consider is that our behavior in politics is made possible by the way we view politics. We value politics entirely for what we can get out of it, while holding a low view of what politics itself is and can be. Politics is considered by many as, in its very essence, an area of life that is not just dominated by an amoral, self-centered logic but *intended* to be dominated by that logic. Some approach politics, when they consider it at all, in the same way one might approach a used car dealership: with an aggressive defensiveness, eager to secure one's narrow purpose without much concern for the human beings involved and to get on with "real life" as quickly as possible. It is a place for self-interested consumption, not service. Some with a low, self-interested view of politics approach it as a game one can master, while others with that same view take it as reason to never engage at all, but it all happens under the same cynical political imagination.

WHAT YOU WON'T FIND IN THIS BOOK

Before I move on much further, I want to address a desire that I suspect may be emerging among some readers—the desire for a political accounting that lays out in full detail the array of misguided positions and tactics of the other side, of the opposing political party or our most noxious political leaders. I understand this desire. I could lay out that case.

There are two reasons I'll not do so here: First, this kind of full accounting falls outside the scope of this book. The purpose of this book is not to convince readers that one political party is better than another or that one politician is a bigger threat than another. Those are important arguments. I have made them before, and those debates must be had.

However, part of the problem in our politics right now is that so much of it is motivated and dictated by what social scientists call "negative polarization," which essentially refers to the idea that much of political engagement is motivated by what you're against rather than by what you're for. I will, at times, have to refer to politicians and issues that invoke partisan politics in order to make a point, but my goal is not to adjudicate the partisan contest. You likely already have a view about which party is better or whether we should have a bigger government or a smaller government. Bring those views to the Lord, and ask for his help as you consider those kinds of positions and issues. This book will offer you tools to do so.

That is very much the posture I invite you to take to this book. Our political discourse is full of people and arguments assuring you that you're on the right side, and that for whatever faults your side has, the real danger is posed by your opponents. This book offers you an opportunity to think about the kind of person *you* are, the kind of person *you* want to be, in our politics. Your first instinct, I hope, will be to apply the ideas in this book to yourself and your life, not to search for ammunition to use against political enemies. When I refer to "our politics" or the kind of approach "we" have in our politics, it is not because every single person shares equal responsibility for every ill in our political life. Instead, I use this language to push against the impulse to immediately distance ourselves from what is wrong in our politics. For the sake of our country, for the sake of our politics, we must take responsibility for addressing even that which we did not ourselves cause. We must take responsibility for what we have contributed to, and what we have not, and not rest in the contentment that at least we didn't vote for "that candidate" or at least we don't hold "that view." The importance of taking responsibility will hopefully become clearer to you as we continue.

However, for those for whom this will be helpful, I will state definitively here that our political life has honest disagreement and principled politicians, but it also has malicious and self-serving actors. Our politics has people with different approaches to the same goals of addressing injustice and affirming human dignity, but it also has people who have different, nefarious goals. The choices we make in politics are consequential. The differences we hold are often not value-neutral. Politics has real stakes for real people that require us to take politics seriously. There is a dignity and a burden in holding the office of citizen, and we must not bear it lightly. A vote or position does not need to be a sin for it to be misguided, just as it is possible and evident that a person can be both misguided and unfaithful to God in one's political actions and involvement.

As we move forward, let's look at some of the defining features of our politics. As you read, consider our politics as it is today. You can think about instances in which politicians either supported or undermined the various dynamics covered in this chapter. But think first of your place and role in it all, the ways in which politicians you've supported have contributed to some of the problems we will discuss, and maybe even allow yourself to acknowledge the good that political opponents have contributed where you can find it.

HOW POLITICS AND POLITICIANS ARE VIEWED

In the middle of the twentieth century, American National Election Studies developed a trust index that measures the level of Americans' trust in government by asking four questions regarding (1) how often respondents believe they can trust government to do what is right, (2) whether government is run by a few big interests looking out for themselves or in the interest of and for the benefit of all, (3) the extent to which people in government waste money that comes from taxpayers, and (4) the prevalence of crooked government officials. When the trust index debuted in 1958, the average score on the index was 49. In the years after Watergate and the Vietnam War, it dropped as low as 29. Since 2008, the trust index dropped to new lows in 2012 (22) and 2016 (17), and the average index score stayed at 17 in 2020.[1]

A Pew Research study found similarly low levels of trust in government, as only 28 percent of American adults said they trust the government in Washington to "do the right thing" "just about always" or "most of the time," a result that has been more or less consistent since the turn of the last century. The same Pew study also found that 65 percent of Americans believe that all (15 percent) or most (50 percent) candidates for public office run in order to pursue their own personal interests. Only 21 percent believe candidates run for office to serve their communities.[2]

This lack of trust in, and esteem for, government and public servants functions not only as a judgment but also as an expectation. Once people assume that politicians are in it for purposes of self-interest and self-aggrandizement, their expectation for what would count as rational behavior from government officials is reshaped to that assumption. Politicians are forced to respond to and act in light of that expectation. Other aspects of our current political culture compound this problem. I do not know if it is possible to have high respect or esteem where trust is low. Low trust is the prerequisite for so many of the behaviors and proclivities that are most decried in our politics today.

POLITICAL SECTARIANISM

Polarization and related issues such as government dysfunction, a lack of willingness to compromise, and broader and deeper forms of social division are widely recognized as problems by both voters and politicians. Yet we've been stuck in a downward spiral of degenerating polarization and dysfunction for decades.

As noted in the introduction, in October 2020, fifteen scholars from a range of fields came together to issue a dire warning: "A poisonous cocktail of othering, aversion and moralization poses a threat to democracy." In a brief essay,[3] these scholars report the kind of polarization that has emerged is of a different nature than that which preceded it. Political disagreement is not itself a symptom of political dysfunction; in fact, it can be a sign of a healthy politics. The polarization we have today, though, focuses "less on triumphs of ideas than on dominating the abhorrent supporters of the opposing party." The scholars offer an interdisciplinary integration of the various insights that have resulted from this research to develop and name a framework that describes the kind of polarization we have today: "political sectarianism." Political sectarianism is "the tendency to adopt a moralized identification with one political group and against another."[4]

Political sectarianism is upheld by three pillars: *othering*, which is "the tendency to view opposing partisans as essentially different or alien to oneself"; *aversion*, "the tendency to dislike and distrust opposing partisans"; and *moralization*, "the tendency to view opposing partisans as iniquitous" as opposed to merely wrongheaded.[5]

What does political life look like when it runs on the fuel of aversion, othering, and a misplaced moralization? "Democrats and Republicans have grown more contemptuous of opposing partisans for decades, and at similar rates. Only recently, however, has this aversion exceeded their affection for co-partisans . . . Out-party hate has become more powerful than in-party love as a predictor of voting behavior."[6]

The authors continue: "This aversion to opposing partisans might make strategic sense if partisan identity served as a strong proxy for political ideas. But given that sectarianism is not driven primarily by such ideas, holding opposing partisans in contempt on the basis of their identity alone precludes innovative cross-party solutions and mutually beneficial compromises."[7] In other words, political hatred has become so profound that it outstrips many individuals' desire to actually help themselves, not to mention loftier motivations like pursuing the common good. Political sectarianism is a state in which we hate our opponents so much that we'll do harm to ourselves and our interests before we concede anything to them.

The consequences of this political sectarianism are serious, including "immediate links to governance," such as a compromising of political representation, the incentivizing of antidemocratic tactics, and the undermining of government competency. This political antipathy reaches into our interpersonal and social lives, as political sectarianism has "increased the social distance between Democrats and Republicans."[8] A 2020 study published in the *American Political Science Review* found the American public's ability to check undemocratic behaviors among politicians to be "strikingly limited," as only 3.5 percent of Americans would cast ballots against their preferred candidates in response to undemocratic behavior.[9] Milan Svolik, a coauthor of the study, explained: "Our findings show that US voters, regardless of their party affiliation, are willing to forgive undemocratic behavior to achieve their partisan ends and policy goals. *We find that polarization raises the stakes of elections and, in turn, the price of prioritizing democratic principles over partisan interests.*"[10]

Again, the problem with the kind of polarization we have today is not that Americans and our various political parties disagree. Disagreement can be healthy. Our politics needs disagreement. The purpose of politics is to mediate it. Some ideas and policies really are bad and deserve both disagreement and defeat. However, political sectarianism is about much more than disagreement.

Political sectarianism demands a constant state of conflict, and so politics becomes a forum for antagonism rather than public service. It's one thing for politicians to approach our politics in this way, to never stop campaigning; it's another for citizens to view politics as a stage for animosities and resentments. This is a critical development. We're all either political strategists or political cynics now. Our expectation of the worst in our politics turns into a willingness to excuse and rationalize it. Motivated by disdain for the "other side," as well as a belief that our opponents will do anything to win, partisans demand that their politicians do whatever necessary so that they might win. This, of course, only fuels greater division and animosity.

Note again that the framework of political sectarianism is not consumed with an analysis of specific policy views. The pillars that hold up political sectarianism (aversion, othering, and moralization) do not describe policy differences or distinctions, but rather how we relate to and think about one another. Political sectarianism obscures distinctions among those who belong to the same political party or are otherwise viewed to adhere to a common political cause. We become unable to see the differences among those who disagree with us; they congeal into an enemy that simply must be defeated. The logic of political sectarianism suggests that policy difference must be expressed through antisocial behavior or else you don't really believe it. Political sectarianism creates a culture that conflates conviction with anger, belligerence, and antagonism.

POLITICAL PARTIES AND THEIR PURPOSE

Political sectarianism runs its course through and within the framework of political parties. Political parties ought to serve as vehicles for mediating differences, first within a party and then between the parties themselves. Instead, we have allowed parties to become brands and sources of identity. We have allowed them to become masters when they are meant to be servants.

Because our parties are so polarized and party identity is so profound, we find that politicians and political parties have inordinate influence over the views of the citizenry.[11] We have not invested such meaning into what a political party is and what it means to affiliate with one because of the nature of a political party but because of what is in the interest of political parties and other political actors who benefit from them. That is to say, political parties demand our allegiance not because it is their right but because it is in their interest. *We should be members of a political party because we believe things; we should not believe things because we are members of a political party.*

However, this approach would not be in the immediate interests of our political parties, particularly those individuals with the most power in those parties, or those interests that are currently most favored and privileged by the political party. These individuals and interests want to deepen and solidify their hold on the party and the power it offers. There are at least two ways they can do that: by convincing members of a party that loyalty requires they change their views to be in line with what party leadership currently wants, or by promoting a situation in which party loyalty is motivated more significantly by opposition to the other party than by positive affirmation of their own party. Both strategies keep the pressure off the party to reflect on and manage intraparty disagreements.

Political sectarianism changes what we think politics is for and what is appropriate in our politics. Incivility, vulgarity, and indecency are now tools in the political toolbox that are deemed useful in the pursuit of political victory or some policy end. People are willing to go on the record with these views.

On July 17, 2019, *The New York Times* ran an article with the headline "With Name-Calling and Twitter Battles, House Republican Campaign Arm Copies Trump's Playbook."[12] The article described a concerted, strategic effort to "alienate swing voters by tagging all House Democrats as socialists, anti-Semites, or far-left extremists." This was done by popularizing and institutionalizing name-calling and epithets. A moderate Democrat,

Max Rose, who served in the military and was awarded a Purple Heart, was tagged in digital attacks as "Little Max Rose."

From the article:

> Republican campaign operatives backing the strategy argued that aggressive tactics were necessary to rouse the interests of sleepy and shrunken local press corps. Adopting the mantra that "all news is good news," the committee appears to believe that even if reporters choose instead to write about its bare-knuckled tactics, they are at least reiterating the nicknames and points that House Republicans hope will reach voters.
>
> "If that's what it takes to get a story," said Mike Shields, who joined the National Republican Congressional Committee as director of its independent expenditure program in 2009 and helped Republicans win a 63-seat gain. "There needs to be a shift in mind-set to be in the majority. It's better than getting no coverage at all."
>
> Some Republican members have pushed back, expressing disappointment and disapproval of the personal attacks, but the NRCC continues to defend their tactics.

Not long after this article was published, the newspaper reported on the internal debate within the Democratic Party infrastructure about whether to try to respond in kind when it came to digital advertising.[13] The article reports that "Democrats are struggling to match more than the sheer volume of content coming out of the Trump campaign. Interviews with Democratic consultants and experts revealed a party deeply hesitant to match the Trump campaign's intense and often angry partisan approach."

The story went on to cite anonymous Democratic staffers

who were upset that senior staff had rejected their attempts to air aggressive, divisive ads meant to "fire up the base." One Democratic digital strategist was willing to go on the record: "Republicans are not messaging around unity and civility because those things don't mobilize people." She added that while everyone may want to live in a less divided country, "nobody takes time off work, gets in their car, and drives to the polls to vote specifically for that." Another strategist explained, "There's an algorithmic bias that inherently benefits hate and negativity and anger."

Do you see it? The challenges in our politics are not systemic to the exclusion of the personal and individual. Instead, many of our most profound political problems reflect how our political institutions' process and respond to the habits of the heart that are held, fundamentally, at the level of the individual. These habits are acted on at all levels of human life, including at the level of personal relationships, the immediate community, and our broader political and public life. *We are in a vicious feedback loop of a citizenry that makes itself available for and incentivizes political tactics that degrade people and degrade our politics, which leads to a normalization or routinization—an embeddedness—of these kinds of political tactics and approaches.*

MODES OF ENGAGEMENT

The most engaged, most ideological segments of the American electorate are the wealthiest segments of the American electorate. In a report stemming from extensive research, More in Common describes an American electorate that is made up of seven "tribes."[14] The most strident of these tribes are what More in Common terms the "Devoted Conservatives" and the

"Progressive Activists." They are the least open to compromise, the most certain of the morality and rightness of their political views. They are also the wealthiest and whitest of More in Common's seven tribes. Devoted Conservatives and Progressive Activists are the only two tribes in which a majority of members have a household income of more than $50,000—and more than a fifth of each have a household income of more than $100,000. Together, they account for 14 percent of the American public, though because they are the most engaged in our politics, they have an outsized influence on the shape and nature of our political culture.

We'll return to describing More in Common's tribes, but it's important here to introduce another concept—political hobbyists. The term comes from political scientist Eitan Hersh, who explains that *political hobbyist* is a "catchall term for the person who spends a lot of time consuming news or signing online peti tions or engaging online with people about this or that issue. They mistake this for actual politics, but it's not because it doesn't contribute to power-building."[15] Hersh's concept of political hobbyists doesn't overlay directly onto More in Common's tribes, but it helps us consider the kinds of contributions and modes of engagement that people bring to our politics.

In an interview with Sean Illing for *Vox*, Hersh continues to explain that the prototypical political hobbyist will follow the latest national political controversy and know the ins and outs of all of that intrigue, yet "if you asked him how he could get involved on some issues of importance in his local community or in his state, or where the pressure points are in his community to influence government, he has no idea. He's just caught up in the national news cycle and he's not actually improving anything."[16]

Moreover, while the hobbyist's imagination for politics is

cultivated by Twitch streams, clips of shows like *The Daily Show*, and Twitter threads, these forms of content are only distantly related to the actual work of politics.[17] Hersh explains, "Online politics is all about provocation and signaling outrage. But changing people's minds, turning your vote into many votes, requires empathy and face-to-face engagement. Not only are you not doing this online or when watching cable news, you're learning exactly the wrong skill set."[18]

Political hobbyism is a problem because political hobbyists "are making politics worse." Eitan Hersh explains, "Our collective treatment of politics as if it were a sport affects how politicians behave. They increasingly believe they benefit from feeding the red meat of outrage to their respective bases, constantly grandstanding for the chance that a video of themselves will go viral. In treating politics like a hobby, we have demanded they act that way."[19] Hersh continues, "Hobbyism is a serious threat to democracy because it is taking well-meaning citizens away from pursuing power. The power vacuum will be filled."[20]

The average citizen is not a political hobbyist. Political hobbyists are one category of people who, in general, find in politics a form of entertainment, a method of gaining emotional satisfaction. Yet there are others who reject politics, understandably, because they do not find emotional satisfaction in it. In both cases, it is one's emotional satisfaction that is far too determinative of whether and how one approaches politics.

Which brings us back to More in Common's tribes. Two-thirds of Americans belong to typologies of tribes that are part of what More in Common calls the "Exhausted Majority." The Exhausted Majority is made up of four tribes—Moderates, Traditional Liberals, the Politically Disengaged, and Passive Liberals—and comprises 67 percent of the American electorate.[21]

These Americans are less attached to the narratives promoted by political sectarianism, but they are fatigued by our politics and feel unheard by those in power. When those who are most engaged treat politics as a game, others who are less engaged are led to view politics as a game as well, which only serves to reinforce their decision to avoid politics. It is understandable that people who face so much in their lives that is dehumanizing, undignifying, and embarrassing choose to limit their exposure to a politics of derision. People have to deal with enough drama in their own immediate social reality; a politics that seems to thrive off of drama and conflict, and demand toxic behavior from those who participate in it, doesn't seem all that attractive to many people. I get it. I suspect others observe our politics and determine that if taking politics seriously requires them to become a jerk or a sycophant, they'll pass. The problem, though, is not that political hobbyists take politics too seriously but that they take politics seriously in all the wrong ways.

These are some of the kinds of people in our politics: the Exhausted and Detached, the Entertained Consumer, the Angry and Certain. But there are other ways of approaching politics. Even among those we might think would fall into these categories, their contribution need not be entirely negative. We have something to learn from the Exhausted, and we have something to learn from the Angry. That said, these modes of engagement fall far short of any ideal for both our politics and our souls.

Positive, service-oriented approaches to politics are possible in this environment, but when we see people who approach politics this way, we are surprised. We are suspicious. We view these people as impossibly heroic or hopelessly naive. The true public servant is viewed in a way that is not all that dissimilar from the saint.

HOW CHRISTIANS VIEW POLITICS

Years ago, I was speaking at a church in New York City. Following the event, a woman approached me to express her appreciation for my remarks. She was relieved to hear that someone was trying to be faithful while working in politics, but "it must be so difficult," she said. Politics is full of compromises, and the incentives in politics do not reward faithfulness, but winning. "I don't really know how you do it," she said, "but I'm glad you're out there trying." We continued in conversation until at one point I asked her about her job. She replied, "Oh, I work on Wall Street."

Politics is not uniquely challenging to faithfulness, even as there are unique challenges to faithfulness in politics. This is no different, though, from the challenges facing schoolteachers or salespeople, stay-at-home parents or, yes, those who work on Wall Street. Fundamentally, for those who work in politics and for all of us as citizens, the call in politics is to steward the responsibility we have, in the midst of difficult and complex circumstances, for the glory of God and the good of our neighbors.

Some Christians excuse immorality in politics because they have a "low" view of politics. They think immorality is acceptable in politics because it is inherently corrupt, and a moral approach to politics is unthinkable to them, even as they emphasize morality in other areas of life. Others excuse immorality in politics because they have a "high" view of politics. They place such importance on political outcomes that they believe immoral conduct is justified, even necessary, for the greater good.

Whether politics is seen as "higher" or "lower," Christianity is considered ill-equipped and irrelevant to the "practical" task at hand. Politics is where real decisions are made, and Jesus' teachings are not viewed highly for their executive functions.

There are votes to win and candidates to elect. If there is a Christian call to kindness, for instance, we dare not take that call into politics, lest we make a fool of ourselves, consigning ourselves to irrelevancy. Christianity then becomes a hindrance toward getting what we want, what we think we need, from our politics.

It may be the case that very few Christians will come right out and say that they believe the way of Jesus is inadequate in politics, but I want you to consider whether it might make sense of much of present-day reality if we take that to be the case.

POLITICAL THERAPEUTIC DEISM

Not only is our politics shaping who we are as individuals, but it's also shaping our churches. In the next chapter, we'll explore one of the primary ways to understand how and why this is the case, but before we do, it's important to wrap our arms around the severity of the problem.

One pastor described it to me this way. Fifteen years ago, he knew when he received an email from someone new to the church asking for a meeting, the person most likely wanted to know the pastor's views on salvation, hell, the problem of evil, or other doctrinal issues. Now when he receives an email asking for a meeting, he goes to the meeting expecting that the person he's meeting with doesn't want to know anything about the pastor's views on the Bible or what he studied in seminary. Instead, he's asked who he voted for in the last election or what he thinks about a particular hot-button political issue.

The sociologists Christian Smith and Melinda Lundquist Denton introduced the term "Moral Therapeutic Deism" in their 2005 book *Soul Searching: The Religious and Spiritual Lives of American Teenagers*. Moral Therapeutic Deism (MTD) describes a dominant system of beliefs the researchers found among adolescents at the time through thousands of interviews.[22] The research rightly sparked concern among many, particularly conservative Christians, since MTD is made up of beliefs that are not necessarily Christian but seem to fit comfortably into the culture of many churches and "Christian" homes.[23]

In a conversation with Dallas Willard, John Ortberg defines MTD this way: "Whether or not somebody would put themself in the Christian or 'other' category, [MTD] is the kind of prevailing idea about God, and the notion is there is a God; God does exist. He wants everybody to be nice; that's the moralistic part. He wants me to feel good about myself; that's the therapeutic part. And he's available if I need him in a crisis, but other than that, I really don't have to think about him much, and he doesn't want to and will not interfere with my life."[24] MTD offers a God who will not interfere with real life except to the extent that the God of MTD affirms a person's moral goodness and destiny.

It is true that politics is causing spiritual harm in this country, and a big reason for that is people are going to politics to get their spiritual needs met.[25] What is also true is that people are going to church to get their political views affirmed. It was conventional wisdom, especially among evangelicals, that churches that prioritized politics would inevitably die out because people can get their political fix elsewhere. We do see evidence of this. However, we are also observing the power of religious expressions that sanction and anoint people's political views.

It is Political Therapeutic Deism, a kind of religious perspective that exists to offer divine affirmation of one's politics. It is made up of these kinds of beliefs:

1. God is on my political party's side.
2. My views on political issues are a leading indicator that I am a true Christian.
3. My actions in politics are justified in light of God's general approval of my politics.
4. I do not understand how other "Christians" could vote for my candidate's opponent.
5. It is clear and obvious which political issues are most important to God.

Political Therapeutic Deism makes sense of why we're seeing sorting in our churches by politics, over and above theology or other factors. It makes sense of why we've seen steep declines of religious affiliation among Democrats over the last several decades, and why Trump supporters identify as evangelical, even if they don't share evangelicals' theological beliefs.[26] It makes sense of political scientist Michele Margolis's contention that politics influences our religious identities and that partisan forces are responsible for shaping religious divides along partisan lines.[27] It is why a pastor who is merely reading the assigned Scripture from the lectionary can be accused of partisan motive if the Scripture happens to run crosswise of the political needs of the moment. God, Scripture, theological precepts—these are often not desired to refine one's politics, but rather to provide supplemental support for one's politics. It's why they are valued.

Accordingly, while the twentieth century saw the rise of seeker-sensitive churches within evangelicalism, we are seeing "politics-sensitive churches" in our day. Churches are attracting and losing members on the basis of their political appeals, or lack thereof.

In a 2022 article in *The Atlantic*, Tim Alberta, the son of an evangelical pastor, pointed to a church in his hometown, FloodGate Church, where the pastor preached to a congregation of about one hundred people for a decade until in 2020, he took a political stand, defying local emergency shutdown orders from the Michigan government to hold an in-person, indoor church service on Easter. Within a year, the church had fifteen hundred regular attendees.

"Between 40 minutes of praise music and 40 minutes of preaching is the strangest ritual I've ever witnessed inside a house of worship," Alberta explains. The pastor "calls it his 'diatribe.' The congregants . . . call it something else: 'Headline News.' . . . For the next 15 minutes, Bolin does not mention the forgiveness of sins, the resurrection of the body, or the life everlasting."[28] Instead, the congregants heard politics. And they loved it. They didn't get this at the churches they used to attend—if they attended church at all.

The shaping of religious commitments and communities by partisan forces and motives happens across the political spectrum. One of the most ridiculous examples I remember is when the Senate was considering legislation to repeal the Affordable Care Act in 2017. In order for the Republicans' bill to move forward for a vote, the Senate had to have what is called a "motion to proceed" vote, which is exactly what it sounds like—a vote to proceed with consideration of a bill.

One progressive Christian, someone who had served in a leadership position for a Christian organization, shared on social media that he hoped people would leave their churches if their pastor didn't talk about the upcoming "motion to proceed" vote. The motion to proceed vote! First of all, few people have ever heard of a motion to proceed vote. Second, if that vote succeeded, the whole point is that it would be followed by a vote on the actual bill. I presume this individual would then want every pastor of every church attended by his social media followers to speak about that vote.

For many, to do politics is to issue threats, to accuse, to turn policy disagreement or uncertainty into an entrenched marker of character and motives. That approach is then brought to the church, and the local church becomes just one more arena in which to advocate and campaign.

Many people want Christianity and churches to (re)enforce their politics, and the corollary of this is that they do not want God to mess with their politics.

Our political culture is both infecting the culture of our churches and making it more difficult to see the ways our faith can help us reject and renew our toxic politics. The very antidote our faith provides is made anathema because it threatens what we really, actually trust.

THIS IS WHERE WE ARE

This account only skims the surface of our political disrepair. Our response to the state of our politics tips toward distancing ourselves from it—turning up our nose or throwing up our hands. We must not do this.

We must not do it because politics is important. We literally cannot do away with it. Wherever there are people in community, there will be politics. As citizens in political communities with representative systems of government, not only are we affected by our politics, but we also have a responsibility for it. We should also recognize the tremendous good that government does and that our political process produces, even now.

There are real structural problems with our democracy, and neither the popular will nor our individual wills are perfectly translated in our politics. Yet the structural issues are not completely removed from the will of citizens, from that which we promote, desire, and allow. We must be willing to take the responsibility that is ours.

The Christian's responsibility for our politics is special, but not because Christians are or should be privileged by law or because America is a "Christian nation." For too long, Christians have asserted special status for this country, all while avoiding special responsibility. We share with our fellow citizens— Christians and others—the responsibility in and for our politics in the eyes of the law. Yet Christians are also called by God to be a blessing to the cities and nations in which we've been placed. This calling does not bestow special status or privilege; it is a call to service.

And we have much to offer. The logic of our politics is suffocating. It eats away at so much of what a healthy society requires—trust, solidarity, compassion. Truth is discarded when inconvenient, and moral judgments become subject to partisan motives. Political leadership requires moral authority, yet moral claims have been so misused that Americans are questioning the authority of the moral.

Dallas Willard understood our predicament and the significant challenge the misuse of moral claims presents to all of human affairs. His articulation of how this quandary came to be will help us chart a path forward, and it is the subject of our next chapter.

Chapter 2

THE DISAPPEARANCE OF MORAL KNOWLEDGE

On January 6, Jacob Chansley, known as Jake Angeli or the "QAnon Shaman," called for prayer. Just days later, he would be charged for violent entry and disorderly conduct on the grounds of the US Capitol. In the days that followed, he would admit guilt and sign a statement of offense detailing his crimes.[1]

In this moment, however, he was riding high. He felt like the Capitol building was his. He was part of a mob that physically assaulted law enforcement officials and terrorized public servants. Wearing a headdress with horns, he strode down the aisle of the Senate chamber, where others would rummage through Senate desks, hang from the walls, and otherwise seek to defile the meeting place of the "world's greatest deliberative body." Another man shouted, "I invoke the name of Jesus Christ," which gave Chansley an idea.

The New Yorker's Luke Mogelson described the scene this way:

In the Senate chamber on January 6th, Jacob Chansley took off his horns and led a group prayer through a megaphone,

23

from behind the Vice-President's desk. The insurrectionists bowed their heads while Chansley thanked the "heavenly Father" for allowing them to enter the Capitol and "send a message" to the "tyrants, the communists, and the globalists." Joshua Black, the Alabaman who had been shot in the face with a rubber bullet, said in his YouTube confession, "I praised the name of Jesus on the Senate floor. That was my goal. I think that was God's goal."[2]

This raises the question: Was their goal actually God's goal? Was God's will done on January 6?

The Senate chamber itself speaks to this aspiration of aligning one's actions with God's will. I was reminded of this when I saw a photo of one of the insurrectionists hanging from the wall of the Senate chamber, half blocking an inscription of the Latin phrase *annuit coeptis*, or "God has favored our undertakings." This, too, is a kind of prayer. It was inscribed there by people with no ability to see the future, only the desire for those who would work in that place to know they worked not just before men but before God. The inscription expresses a hope that those public servants who have the honor of working in the Senate would conduct themselves in light of that fact. Our politics is judged not by votes alone but by God.

The expectation that "God has favored our undertakings" hangs over our politics and our lives, even when we do not look up to see it. But let's be clear—we look up quite a bit in our public life. One of the great misnomers of our time, repeated by Christians and non-Christians alike, is that we live in a "post-Christian" society. America is not post-Christian. Not demographically. Not culturally.

We should resist centering this idea that America is post-

Christian because of what it implies about our past, present, and future. In reference to the past, to say that America is post-Christian implies there was some point in the past when this country was thoroughly or sufficiently Christian, which naturally raises the question, "When exactly was that?" When was America Christian such that we are now post-Christian? Was America Christian during Jim Crow but not after? During slavery but not after?

We should also reject the notion that America is post-Christian because of what it implies for our present. It is a political provocation, intended by one side to marginalize Christians and by another to mobilize Christians. It is used by those who wish to limit Christian influence to arbitrarily mark the present as definitionally precluding Christian influence, and it is used by those seeking to mobilize Christians as an explanation for everything that is wrong with America. *Why isn't America working? Christians don't have influence like they once did.*

The conversation about whether America is post-Christian or not is rarely an edifying one. We do not need America to be post-Christian to be inclusive. America can be a pluralistic nation, and not be post-Christian. What does it mean to say America is post-Christian when a majority of Americans, including a vast majority of US federally elected political leaders, identify as Christian? Yes, American society is changing, but to say we are post-Christian concedes too much. When applied to the present, it is too often used by Christians to shift blame or avoid responsibility. When applied to the present, it is too often used by those who seek to limit Christian influence to preempt a debate before it can even begin.

Finally, to say America is post-Christian suggests our future is written for us. The claim that America is post-Christian assumes our past, negates our present, and prejudges our future.

The truth is that Christianity is in the mix, as it always has been. Something has changed, certainly, and we'll discuss that in this chapter, but the language of post-Christian has become counterproductive. Christianity was not as hegemonic in the past as some seem to think, and Christianity is not as irrelevant today as we are supposed to believe. This is a time of cultural contestation rather than cultural domination. It would be a mistake to equate a lack of Christian dominance with an absence of Christian influence. Every "God bless America" that ends a speech, every invocation of Scripture, every proclamation that one is on the "right side of history," every declaration of one's favored policy as right or just—these are all, to varying degrees, echoing a hope: that God has favored our undertakings, that he approves of our conduct. But now this is a hope for which many believe there is no accountability, no substance, no reliable knowledge. It is a precarious hope—a hope without basis.

The matter of whether Christians have anything to offer our politics is contested by both Christians and non-Christians. As religious disaffiliation has increased in this country, a greater number of Americans believe Christianity doesn't have much to offer. In fact, Christianity, and religion generally, is increasingly viewed in America as part of the problem as opposed to part of the solution.[3] Perhaps it is not surprising that the nonreligious would doubt the contributions religion has to make to our politics, but, of course, we must keep in mind how often the nonreligious seek to leverage historically religious ideas and resources when it seems desirable to do so.[4]

Furthermore, a significant number of Christians do not think much of what Christianity has to offer the public. Some Christians wrongly, but not without merit, look at all the ways Christianity has been misused in our politics and conclude that the most reliably safe way to proceed is to enact a secular politics. Other Christians have a predominantly private conception of faith that is divorced from knowledge and cannot readily identify what, if any, implications their faith might have for politics. And so we end up with a sloganeering of Scripture or religious phrases during election season or in response to political news of the day, citations of 2 Chronicles 7:14 that serve as the foundation for worship events that pose as political rallies that pose as worship events.

While news of political malfeasance might earn a sighed response of "they need Jesus," the words say less than the easy detachment that underlies them. These kinds of statements are a way of distancing oneself from the work of politics, not actually engaging in it. Whether it's a Christian perspective that withdrawal and disengagement are the best we can do or a Christian sloganeering that is more about an expressive affiliation than it is about content or character, a crisis of confidence lies under it all.

This crisis of confidence, which affects Christians as well as American society at large, is tied to what Dallas Willard has called the "disappearance of moral knowledge."

WHAT IS MORAL KNOWLEDGE?

Jerry Seinfeld once joked that *head* and *cheese* are two words that should never be together. To modern ears, the words *moral* and *knowledge* seem much the same way. The moral relativism that was of such concern to "Christian worldview" experts in the 1990s is clearly not the dominant force in America's present or future. Our public square is full of moral assertions. Dallas Willard made a more precise diagnosis: our moral assertions lack authority; they remain mere assertions, not knowledge.

Moral assertions are used to coerce, to bully, and to protect, and so they are considered to carry as much weight as the power that backs them, but the spirit of our age is one that does not consider morality to be a matter of responding to, or corresponding with, reality.

"Throughout history," Willard writes, "it has been *knowledge*—real or presumed—that was invoked to provide a place to stand in opposing, correcting, and refining moral and immoral traditions and practices."[5]

He continues, "What characterizes life in so-called Western societies today, however, is the *absence*, or presumed absence, of *knowledge* of good and evil, right and wrong, virtue and vice: *knowledge that might serve as a rational basis for moral decisions, for policy enactments and for rational critique of established patterns of response to moral issues.*"[6]

In *The Disappearance of Moral Knowledge*, Willard identifies six causes for the disappearance.

First, because of the historical tie between religion and morality, as "religion itself eventually came to be relocated from the domain of knowledge to that of 'faith,' morality was assumed to follow."[7] As humans' relationship to religion became increasingly viewed as a private and personal affair, cordoned off from contributing as a source of knowledge, talking about morality became more and more challenging. This is particularly true in nations and communities that are predominantly religious, at least historically, as the moral views of their people were informed by religion. If religion is not a source of publicly available knowledge and if most people's views of morality are informed by religion, then public discussion and action based on moral concepts become nonsensical. Morality becomes just a matter of one's own opinion, subject to personal experience if anything, but certainly not the subject of broadly applicable, publicly available knowledge that can and should guide human affairs.

Second, Willard points to the "disappearance of the human self from acceptable domains of knowledge."[8] Here, Willard refers to Empiricism, followed by a series of other developments, particularly in the field of psychology, such that the "self" increasingly became viewed as "governed by unconscious and irrational forces" and therefore not subject to moral knowledge. When the existence of the human will is called into question, the foundations for the consideration of morality become uncertain. Some people would much rather, as a matter of their will, debate the existence of the will than the contours and obligations of morality. Yet it is the existence of the will that is integral to any full accounting of what justice entails and to the dignity of the human person.

Third, Willard describes how the increasing awareness of differences regarding morality across cultures led to a discomfort with and ultimately a negligence of objective moral distinctions and valuations. If there is no moral knowledge, there is no basis for making determinations about what is good, better, and best when it comes to various cultural differences. "The 'disappearance of moral knowledge' thus resolves a range of thorny issues, and that has seemed to make it a quite acceptable state of affairs."[9] If morality is not a matter of knowledge but rather of private practice and preference, we can avoid the messy business of the comparative evaluation of different conceptions of what is moral.

Fourth, moral standards became seen as "power plays," and those who held to them became viewed as "blind or hypocritical."[10] According to this perspective, moral standards do not become moral standards because they are right, but because that standard can be enforced with the backing of sufficient power. It is power that matters, and morality is either a tool of hypocrites or the delusion of those foolish enough to acquiesce to an assertion of power deceptively presented as a matter of morality. Moral standards, then, are viewed as a soft form of coercion, a way to get people to act according to someone else's interests. This view developed, at least in part, as a protective response against the misuse of moral claims and impositions. It is critical to acknowledge that much of this misuse, historically and presently, has derived from Christians and Christian institutions.

Fifth, and relatedly, is the view that morality itself is harmful. This usually goes along with a punitive view of morality, that a moral standard amounts to a senseless "set of rules" that, when not followed, justifies abuse or punishment.[11] Willard describes the view that moral standards are harmful as a rational response to the dominant "Victorian" form of morality in the twentieth century. Also relevant here is what is now referred to as "respectability politics," which generally refers to rules of accepted affect and presentation that can obscure and deflect from greater and deeper moral questions, typically to the benefit of the powerful. A morality of such blatant convenience for some and unjustified punishment for others undermined morality entirely, to the extent that "freedom *from* morality came to be thought of as desirable in many quarters."[12] Here again, actions and systems developed by Christians and Christian institutions play a significant role.

Finally, a fear or resentment of knowledge itself contributed to the disappearance of moral knowledge. "Anything that is allowed to stand as knowledge," Willard explains, "is something that you *must* come to terms with—if not because you respect it as such in the guidance of your life, then at least because others do, and therefore will not leave you alone to disregard it. Knowledge . . . confers right to act, and to direct action and policy, in a way that feeling, opinion (no matter how widely shared), and tradition do not. That proves to be highly threatening to some primary values of contemporary Western life: self-determination and freedom from social domination, for example."[13] When you know something, you can't make yourself unknow it. It informs your outlook and influences your actions. You might wish you could flap your arms and fly, but once you know about gravity, your desire to jump off a cliff and fly will take a back seat to your knowledge that it just won't work. And thank goodness for that!

This is obviously a cursory look at how the disappearance of moral knowledge developed, but it is, I hope, sufficient for our purposes. Before we move on, I'll make just a few connections between these lines of argument from Dallas Willard that are especially relevant to this book.

First, notice that the disappearance of moral knowledge is not solely, or even primarily, driven by completely "secular" forces or by individuals who would have claimed to not believe in God. Willard never intended for consideration of this concept to become one more talking point for the culture wars. We are identifying a development that must be addressed in order to help people.

Second, notice that the disappearance of moral knowledge developed in response to factors that were profoundly imbued with moral intuitions and even convictions. Any defense of morality must, as a matter of efficacy and of morality itself, contend with the kinds of objections Willard acknowledges in his discussion of the development of the disappearance of moral knowledge, including the misuses of moral knowledge described above.

Third, notice the interplay between moral knowledge and public life. Moral knowledge itself has inherent and direct implications for our politics and public life, while the disappearance of moral knowledge came about, in part, due to public pressures. There is a necessary connection between moral knowledge and public life. Moral knowledge is not cultivated by the development of merely private religious beliefs as such, and the causes for the disappearance of moral knowledge are not reducible to the collapse of religious adherence, at least as it is commonly understood.

AN ILLUSTRATION

In the opening pages of *The Divine Conspiracy*, Dallas Willard relates a story from Robert Coles, a leading academic and author who served as Harvard University's professor of psychiatry and medical humanities.[14] Coles wrote an essay in *The Chronicle of Higher Education* titled "The Disparity between Character and Intellect,"[15] which begins with a reference to a commencement address Ralph Waldo Emerson delivered at Harvard in 1837, which argued that "character is higher than intellect." For Coles, Emerson's concern was for the "limits of knowledge and the nature of a college's mission."

This is the concern Coles heard more than 150 years later when a female student came to visit him. The student came from a "working class background," and so she worked her way through college, which included cleaning the rooms of her classmates as a side business. She repeatedly encountered classmates who were rude, including one male classmate who repeatedly propositioned her for sex. This classmate was a high-achieving premed student with whom she had shared two "moral reasoning" courses in which she was sure he had received A's. Yet "look at how he behaves with me, and I'm sure with others," she told Coles. In response to these kinds of encounters, the student had quit her job and was planning to leave Harvard.

Coles listened to her account of college life but could offer no meaningful response to the student's searing indictment. At one point, she said, "I've been taking all these philosophy courses, and we talk about what's true, what's important, what's *good*. Well, how do you teach people to *be* good? . . . What's the point of *knowing* good if you don't keep trying to *become* a good person?"

Coles could not muster much of a response: "Schools are schools, colleges are colleges, I averred, a complaisant and smug accommodation in my voice. Thereby I meant to say that our schools and colleges these days don't take major responsibility for the moral values of their students, but, rather, assume that their students acquire those values at home. I topped off my surrender to the status quo with a shrug of my shoulders, to which she responded with an unspoken but barely concealed anger."[16]

Coles reflected on the exchange, several years after his essay had been published, and offered several ideas for helping students "take that big step from thought to action," including community service and writing assignments asking students to tell of "particular efforts to honor through action the high thoughts we were discussing."[17]

Willard points out, however, that Coles "never confronts the fact that he certainly did not tell the students in his courses that they should not treat someone doing menial work with disdain, or that they should not proposition a classmate or anyone else who is cleaning their rooms."[18]

Willard continues, "There were no questions on his tests about these matters. He never deals with the fact that he could not use such questions because no one can now claim to know about such matters. The problem here is less one of connecting character to intellect than one of connecting intellectual to moral and spiritual realities. The trouble is precisely that character is connected with the intellect. The trouble is what is and is not *in* the intellect. Indeed, in the current world of accepted knowledge one can't even *know* the truth of a moral theory or principle, much less a specific rule. . . . One can only know *about* such theories and principles, and think about them in more or less clever ways."[19]

MORAL KNOWLEDGE AS KNOWLEDGE

This illustration helps us understand what is meant by the disappearance of moral knowledge. As Dallas Willard defines it elsewhere, specifically referring to the moral knowledge Christianity has to offer, it is the *"removal of the recognized values and principles of Christian/traditional moral understanding . . . from the domain of the knowledge that must be taught by the knowledge institutions of Western society.* Instead, those values and principles were relocated . . . *into the domain of feelings and cultural traditions*, where they *could not* be taught by the acknowledged institutions of knowledge as a body of knowledge."[20]

Here's the thing: the disappearance of moral knowledge has not led to the disappearance of moral questions or the need to make decisions that implicate morality and judgments about what is good and what is not good. Thus our uncertainty about whether there is any basis for such decision-making results in anxiety, conflict, and disorder. Many of these questions get relegated to the category of personal choice and experience, deemed to be outside of what can be publicly considered or understood.

Moral decisions are, of course, ours to make. No one else will make them for us. What stokes anxiety, conflict, and disorder is the notion that there is no reliable knowledge we can count on and offer for the consideration of others as we make these decisions. Without that, we're left with political gamesmanship, marketing schemes, and power plays.

The female student's classmate was operating from moral judgments. Perhaps he believed it was known and understood that sex is morally innocuous and that asking for sex was like asking for a breath mint. Maybe he believed that consensual sex is moral sex and that no other standards need to be met. Whatever the classmate was thinking—and it seems safe to say he was thinking primarily of himself and his desires—his actions flowed from his thoughts, from what he believed to be real and relevant, as they do for us all.

In 2022, journalist Christine Emba authored *Rethinking Sex*, an insightful and provocative book that explores the current state of sexual relations and expectations, particularly among unmarried American adults. The book jacket includes a fascinating assurance: "Christine Emba has a message for women who feel let down by today's sexual culture: 'You're Not Crazy. The Thing You Sense Is Wrong Is Wrong.'"[21]

It is a sad indication of where things stand that this could amount to a powerful statement. Not long ago, many thought that reducing morality to a personal judgment, a feeling with no real external validation or grounding, would be freeing. This has not turned out to be the case. Instead, one's own sense of right and wrong has been made fragile and difficult to enforce, even in one's own life. This has developed to the point where a book can be marketed to women drowning in a sexual culture of coercion, with its primary appeal to prospective readers being that they can trust their "sense" of what is wrong.

Imagine a textbook in mathematics marketed not with the promise that one will master geometry or be exposed to new concepts that were previously inaccessible, but with the assurance, *You're not crazy. Eight multiplied by eight is sixty-four.* People who take mathematics seriously, who make decisions and take action based on their understanding of mathematics, will not be appealed to so effectively by an affirmation that they know what they know. We do not only *feel* that eight multiplied by eight is sixty-four; we *know* it. The student knew it was wrong to be propositioned by her classmate. She did not ask her professor to affirm that what she "sensed" was wrong was, *in fact*, wrong. If she did, though, could he have answered? Could we?

The view that moral claims rest, ultimately, on one's own personal feelings or the feelings of those involved leads into dangerous territory. If the standards are subjective, so is the enforcement. Without rooting our moral feelings and intuitions in knowledge of moral reality, we're left looking for validation and assurance without which we might forfeit even our right moral intuitions. It's why the book jacket language is so powerful. It stands in the place of so many of the other messages we receive that are intended to reduce what we know to be wrong to the category of mere feeling or perspective.

This works in a different direction as well. Feelings and "perspectives" are used to justify immoral behavior. When a person is convinced morality is subject only to their own sense of (in)justice, they might be led to vandalize the US Capitol (it is the people's house, after all!) and terrorize those who work there.

"What we suffer from to-day," G. K. Chesterton wrote, "is humility in the wrong place. Modesty has moved from the organ of ambition. Modesty has settled upon the organ of conviction; where it was never meant to be. A man was meant to be doubtful about himself, but undoubting about the truth; this has been exactly reversed. Nowadays the part of a man that a man does assert is exactly the part he ought not to assert—himself."[22]

KNOWLEDGE AND FAITH

Deeply tied to, and a part of, the disappearance of moral knowledge is the view that faith has nothing to do with knowledge. Faith has become a kind of self-assertion. When it is stripped of a claim to knowledge, it cannot hold up in the world and cannot be passed from one generation to the next. (Again, the view that faith is opposed to knowledge is not just imposed by the "secular world"; it is accepted and even perpetuated by many Christians.)

In some circles, the testimonies of Christians who claim they "got saved" absent any thought or reason, or even opposed to it, are especially valued. Faith without knowledge is seen as a particularly exceptional gift and blessing. "I just believed" is the mantra, and the impression given is not just that the "moment of conversion" came, quite literally, "out of nowhere," but that the person still believes without their belief making any real sense to them.

Many Christians will also fall back into assurances that their "convictions" are just a matter of "how they were raised," or they may sheepishly explain when pressed that "this is just what my faith teaches." Whatever the intent of these kinds of statements, their effect is to suggest that what Christians believe is not really something with which others must contend. It reduces the faith to family folklore or tribal sentiments.

In this way, Christianity becomes a mere affiliation, and its adherents take part in a culture that may have some emotional or social benefits, but that culture is only to be taken seriously by those within it. The football fan who says their team is headed to the Super Bowl when they have one of the worst records in the league may insist they believe it, but they also don't really want to be challenged to defend that belief. The family that claims that "Nobody has fun like the Funderman family!" makes a categorical claim they will put on the front of their Christmas card, but it's a claim they don't actually wish to defend in a rational sense. Though it is presented as a claim of knowledge, of truth, it is thought to be self-evident that, despite its construction, a claim like that is not meant to be treated as earnest.

This is how faith is treated by many Christians and, of course, by those non-Christians who consider themselves to be tolerant of religion. Yes, Christians believe "Christianity is true" or "Jesus is the Savior," and that really is fine for them. But what is true for Christians is not necessarily true for others. "I can respect and acknowledge a Christian's beliefs as valid and true for them, as long as they can do the same for me and those of other faiths," an open-minded non-Christian might say. Or "I believe in Jesus, but I understand others were raised differently than I was," a tolerant Christian might say. Of course, these kinds of moves evade the actual content of the Christian faith. Is believing in Jesus only advisable if you were raised a certain way? Can you respect a Christian's beliefs if they consider what they believe to be true for you as well?

One of the great challenges to the Christian faith today is the belief that genuine faith is unsupported by reality. A "true believer" is the person who still believes despite all evidence to the contrary; everyone else is paying attention. It would be one thing if this view was dominant just among the nonreligious, but you will find strains of it among Christians themselves, as we've already discussed. Faith becomes a performative act of certainty that one musters up. No wonder there are so many defensive Christians!

Without knowledge as a resource for faith, faith rests on the thing in which one truly has confidence. A person who believes in a knowledge of money but not a knowledge of God will find that the strength of their faith is vulnerable to financial mishap. It was a knowledge of and trust in money that set the foundation of that person's life, and religious conviction only rests on top of that foundation. A person who believes in a knowledge of politics will find that their faith in God is really an expression of their confidence in a particular ideology or political cause (remember Political Therapeutic Deism), and political trials can upend their sense of faith. Knowledge has much to do with trust, and faith has much to do with both.

Jesus did not call his followers to a faith without substance, a faith set against knowledge. Faith may precede or follow knowledge, but a faith set against knowledge is a faith set against trust, and without trust it will be difficult, if not impossible, to proceed very far into discipleship. We know Jesus says we are to love God with all our heart, mind, soul, and strength, but the disappearance of moral knowledge is so pervasive that we read *mind* differently than the others. We understand that our heart, soul, and strength are to be directed toward God, but *mind* somehow reads as a negation. Our desire (heart), capacity (strength), and being (soul) are to be directed toward God for his glory. But there is an implicit notion in some contexts that knowledge (mind) is to be put to the side in exchange for beliefs, which God will give us without any effort or even awareness on our end.

As Dallas Willard points out, a belief is different from knowledge in that it makes no essential claim to reality. The phrase "Well, that is just what you believe," which stupefies many Christians into acquiescence, is quite plausible, while "That is just what you know" sounds, and is, ridiculous. Knowledge places a claim on those who have it and those who do not. This is why, in ways both appropriate and not, we "defer to the experts." We assume they have knowledge that applies not just to themselves but to reality itself. When I take my car to a mechanic, I'm not interested in what they believe about their personal experience with cars. I want the mechanic to apply what they *know* about cars generally to my car specifically.

As Paul recounts his suffering to Timothy, it is his knowledge of the Lord on which he stands: "And of this gospel I was appointed a herald and an apostle and a teacher. That is why I am suffering as I am. Yet this is no cause for shame, because I know whom I have believed, and am convinced that he is able to guard what I have entrusted to him until that day" (2 Timothy 1:11–12). For Paul, the disciples, and the earliest followers of Jesus, and for those who have made tremendous sacrifices up to and including death for the sake of faithfulness, only knowledge—not warm feelings, not mere beliefs absent knowledge—could resource their conduct. Only *knowing* Jesus could explain Peter's willingness to follow Jesus to a cross. Only *knowing* Jesus could make sense of Paul's life and death. Indeed, it is *knowing* Jesus that made possible the counter-cultural and sacrificial public service of so many Christians, by their own testimony, who have stood up for human rights, civil rights, and social justice. And it is in knowledge—knowledge that is sought, knowledge that unfolds—that the Christian is being renewed, "since you have taken off your old self with its practices and have put on the new self, which is being renewed in knowledge in the image of its Creator" (Colossians 3:9–10).

THE SEPARATION OF CHURCH AND STATE

The disappearance of moral knowledge does not result from the separation of church and state, nor does the separation of church and state require the disappearance of moral knowledge. That said, the separation of church and state seems to support the privatization of faith and the dismissal of moral knowledge from public consideration.

The specific phrase "separation of church and state" is not found in the US Constitution, but it was used by Thomas Jefferson and the basic concept derives from constitutional sources such as the First Amendment and Article VI of the Constitution. A narrow reading of the establishment clause, for instance, interprets "Congress shall make no law respecting an establishment of religion" to basically mean there shall be no federal law that would, for instance, make the Evangelical Lutheran Church of America (ELCA) the official denomination of the United States and require the bishop of the ELCA to approve of government actions and laws. Likewise, Article VI's mandate that "no religious Test shall ever be required as a Qualification to any Office or public Trust under the United States" is narrowly interpreted to mean there cannot be a law mandating that a particular position be held by a Christian or Muslim or Hindu.

Broader interpretations of these provisions can lead to

actions across society that are taken to be legally required by the "separation" and its constituent legal and constitutional provisions, such as classifying any entanglement of government funds with religious expression as a form of establishment. This dynamic was at issue in *Rosenberger v. United States*, which considered whether a state university (the University of Virginia) could withhold funds for a religious student publication that would be available to a similar nonreligious publication. Because the University of Virginia is a public school, it operates as an agent of the government, and therefore, the reasoning goes, supporting the publication of a religious publication amounts to government support for religion. Thankfully, the Supreme Court decided that it instead amounted to viewpoint discrimination.

Far more pervasive is how the popular understanding of the separation of church and state can take on a life of its own in the actions and perspectives of leaders of institutions and everyday citizens. When I worked in the White House, we launched an effort to educate our government's own diplomatic corps about religious engagement. This effort was partially in response to reports we had heard from some diplomats who were uncertain of what was allowed and what was prohibited when it came to engaging with religious leaders where they were posted. One diplomat reported they had a policy of not engaging with religious leaders at all because they believed it would be a violation of the separation of church and state. This belief, of course, was not true. Depending on where they were serving, such a perspective could severely undermine their ability to carry out their duties. But the popular understanding of the separation of church and state that was passed down to them, that they imbibed from their education and their professional experience, was that it would be inappropriate for the public sector to engage with religion and religious leaders.

The specter of this legal doctrine affects more than government. I once spoke with a philanthropic leader about the contributions of faith-based organizations to the very causes that her institution supported with its philanthropy. When I finished, the leader told me that while she appreciated the work that faith-based organizations do, her institution could not fund religious groups because of the separation of church and state. I responded, as a friendly rejoinder, "Which one are you?" The leader had no answer. She had not thought about it deeply, even as she stewarded millions of dollars. She had simply received the message that the separation of church and state seems to send and promote, even if it is not a requirement of the principle or intended by all who promote it—namely, that religion is of personal interest at best and not relevant to the public good or appropriate for general consideration or support.

On what basis should secular knowledge be the only source of knowledge for public consideration? Is "Thou shalt not murder" religious knowledge or secular knowledge? What laws inspired by explicitly religious arguments should be declared unconstitutional now? The Civil Rights Act of 1964? Does secular knowledge really suffice for governance?

We should ask the question Dallas Willard asked: "Is reality secular?" Who has determined that and on what grounds?

KNOWLEDGE AND OUR POLITICS

Ahead of the 1960 presidential election, then-Senator John F. Kennedy appeared in front of the Greater Houston Ministerial Association to assure the nation he would not heed directives from the Catholic Church if he were elected as America's first

Catholic president.[23] It was an eleven-minute, workmanlike speech; he was there to make a commitment, and he made it. He declared the central issues of the campaign were "not religious issues." "I believe in a President whose religious views are his own private affair, neither imposed by him upon the nation or imposed by the nation upon him as a condition to holding that office," Kennedy said. "Whatever issue may come before me as President . . . I will make my decision in accordance with these views, in accordance with what my conscience tells me to be the national interest, and without regard to outside religious pressures or dictates. And no power or threat of punishment could cause me to decide otherwise," Kennedy promised.

Kennedy's full meaning can be debated, and his own behavior as president contradicted interpretations of his remarks as calling for a total exclusion of religious influence in political affairs. Indeed, he met with clergy as president and referred to theological concepts on issues like civil rights, nuclear nonproliferation, and a range of other issues. Yet, without too fine a reading of the speech, the basic message the American people heard was that it was inappropriate for religion to have an influence on political decisions.

It appeared that this basic message was embraced across the political and religious spectrum, as Kennedy, a Democrat and a Catholic, gave the speech to appeal to Protestant and other clergy who were heavily Republican. This seemed to be the consensus approach, though that consensus was supported by the confluence of anti-Catholic bigotry and the electoral aspirations of a Catholic running for president. Still, circumstantial as it was, the speech served to further advance the view that religion ought to be a private matter, cordoned off from public life.

"Knowledge is always political," Dallas Willard argued,

"not in its nature or what it is—you can't know by voting or counting votes—but in its effects." He continues, "That knowledge, and perhaps religious knowledge above all, is political follows from the relationship it has to truth, method, evidence, and life . . . because it confers upon the possessor the right and responsibility to act, direct action, set and supervise policy, and teach, it cannot not be political." It is this obvious authority of knowledge that "helps us appreciate why, in Western societies and especially in America, there is such a huge drive to *rule* religion and Christian institutions and teachings *out of the domain of knowledge.* By that move religion is stripped of the rights and responsibilities that always accompany knowledge and that would certainly increase its political influence."[24] If it was generally understood that Christianity offers reliable information that is essential to human life and the flourishing of communities of persons made in the image of God, our politics would have to accommodate itself to that understanding.

Again, neither I nor Willard deny the importance of the separation of church and state as a legal doctrine grounded in the First Amendment. Willard wrote that it should be "zealously upheld."[25] But one concern Willard had regarding politics was its ability to shape what is considered to be *real*, while political decisions are not made on the basis of knowledge. "In time, religion and morality became merely 'political,' as they are now for most people," Willard argued. "What is political, as now understood, does not require knowledge, but only advocacy. Its only issue is how to 'win' for 'your side.'"[26]

In a democracy, what wins constitutes its own kind of reality, which is supported by a political apparatus that responds to that political victory in ways that are not necessarily constrained by a sense of morality or truth. In democratic politics, winning carries its own kind of moral authority, grounded not in knowledge per se, but in the will of the people.

This helps explain why our politics and public life are replete with religious appeals but lack religious accountability. Religious appeals are most commonly made in our politics on the basis of identity, not knowledge. They are essentially commercial appeals intended to reach, cultivate, and win a particular audience, not claims to knowledge that would, first and foremost, serve to hold the communicator accountable. It is in this light that we have greater clarity as to why it seems politics is affecting and shaping our faith more than our faith is shaping our politics. We'll seek to understand more of this dynamic as we proceed.

CONSIDER THE UK

On the right and the left in the United States, it is commonly held that the American approach to religion—the lack of an established church, free exercise, and so forth—made space for a "marketplace of ideas" and is to be credited with America's exceptional rates of religious adherence and practice as compared to Europe. "Europe," it is said, "is full of big, opulent churches, but they are empty. No one worships there anymore. They may have religious rituals, but these are cultural and lack the feeling and spontaneity of American religion. Look at the numbers! Europe clearly has much to learn about Christianity from America." And it may well be that Europe can learn something from the American experience. The sentiment is not entirely wrong.

It's not entirely right though either. I've had the opportunity to travel to Europe a fair amount over the last decade. I've met Christian professors in Prague and attended a thriving evangelical congregation in Bologna. I've spent countless hours in big cathedrals and small neighborhood congregations and have been struck by the humble faithfulness of the people who are there in the pews, as their parents and grandparents and great-grandparents were. I've walked in Cortona and heard the name of Saint Margaret spoken with reverence by schoolboys, and the stories of her faithfulness told as inspiration for action and belief today.

I've spent a significant amount of time in the United Kingdom, where God is moving in tremendous ways through his people, whether it be through Alpha, which has blessed not just the UK but Christian communities around the world, or a growing movement of churches founded by African immigrants. Churches like Holy Trinity Brompton are an inspiration for Christian ministries across the world. InterVarsity traces its roots to a movement of students emerging out of Cambridge University, and the London Institute for Contemporary Christianity (LICC), founded by John Stott, is at the cutting edge of the faith and work movement. The organization I founded, the Center for Christianity and Public Life, takes inspiration from the LICC, as well as the UK-based research think tank THEOS.

The UK has an established church. When Queen Elizabeth died, her stewardship of matters of governance was praised alongside her solemn commitment to defending the faith. Her funeral was presided over by Archbishop Justin Welby, who delivered a sermon that spoke plainly about the reality of the faith that Queen Elizabeth held, which is available to all.[27] When King Charles took the throne, he did so by committing to his role as defender of the faith while also reaffirming "the duty to protect the diversity of our country, including by protecting the space for faith itself and its practice through the religions, cultures, traditions and beliefs to which our hearts and minds direct us as individuals."[28]

On one trip to England, my time there overlapped with the setting of the terms of debate in the House of Lords by Archbishop Welby, as the archbishop does annually. That year, he began a discussion regarding "the shared values underpinning our national life and their role in shaping public policy priorities," and he opened debate with his extended thoughts on the matter.[29] Members of the House of Lords added their perspectives throughout the day. What is communicated by such a practice is not the right of religion to dictate the course of politics through imposition but the propriety and place of religion to contribute to political considerations.

Surely there are other ways for such a view to be advanced in public life and to be held by citizens without an established church or practices like what I witnessed at the House of Lords. I do wonder, though, whether we will one day determine that America's approach to religion contributed not so much to a marketplace where religious knowledge was pursued and could flourish but a marketplace that (as marketplaces do) promoted a consumeristic approach to religion that had less to do with knowledge and more to do with affinity and affiliation.

A BRIEF WORD ON CONCERNS ABOUT MORAL AND RELIGIOUS KNOWLEDGE

As King Charles's remarks quoted above indicate, there is a legitimate and sincere concern that the more seriously religion is taken, the more likely it will be used to harm and coerce. This is one of the primary causes for the disappearance of moral knowledge in the first place, and the concern should be taken seriously. Moreover, in diverse societies, there is the rational concern that a religious majoritarianism will lead to mistreatment of religious minorities.

We will consider the matter of pluralism in greater detail later in this book, but it's necessary to state here that as surely as the religious wars of the sixteenth and seventeenth centuries showed us the evil that could come of bad religious ideas, the destruction of the twentieth century showed us what could come of bad secular ideas. Evil does not need religion as an excuse for evil, though it will use whatever it can. All that presents itself as knowledge is not good, and we are right to be on guard against those who would justify harm and abuse. Of course, moral knowledge is a helpful aid in identifying harm and in preventing wrongdoing. Indeed, it is only with moral knowledge that tolerance, justice, and human dignity can be reliably resourced.

A NEW OPENING

I see a new opening to moral knowledge in our public life, though its sources may surprise some. After decades in which questions of character were deemed to be the province of one political party, the rise and presidency of Donald Trump led to a new conversation about the importance of character and morality in political leaders among many people who once believed character to be largely irrelevant. Perhaps this revitalized interest in character will stick and provide a pathway to a national reconsideration of what it means and requires to be a good person.

The very recognition of cultural diversity that spurred a sort of flattening of the value of moral differences and the

disappearance of moral knowledge is now leading to an appreciation of nonscientific "ways of knowing." Medical schools,
in an effort to promote inclusion of "indigenous perspectives,"
have begun to promote the validity of "ways of knowing" that
are alternative to standard scientific practice.[30] Spiritual health
is recognized as an essential aspect of overall health by organizations like McKinsey,[31] and leading academic institutions and
medical schools have entire centers dedicated to spirituality and
health.[32] Racial diversity within American institutions, as well as
globalization, may contribute to a resurgent recognition of moral
knowledge as well.

Finally, as noted already, relativism is dying. Young people,
especially, have deeply felt moral intuitions. It is exhausting,
unsatisfactory, and largely unproductive to make and hold moral
convictions without grounding or authority. We are already seeing a desire among socially conscious young people to ground
their activism and their earnest impulses in something lasting
and real.[33]

Moral knowledge might make a comeback.

MORAL KNOWLEDGE IS ESSENTIAL

Whether or not there is a renewed public appreciation for moral
knowledge as such, moral knowledge will never be irrelevant.
Our lives run on moral knowledge, or the lack of it. We must
consider the moral in our decision-making because we live in
a moral universe. Therefore, it is vital that we seek to interro-
gate whether our moral feelings are grounded in knowledge.
Unfortunately, because of the denial of moral knowledge
as knowledge, there is this idea that one's moral beliefs are

unassailable and uncontestable. Instead, we should test our moral views and ensure they aren't just the residue of culture or family but are actually grounded in knowledge that can be confidently offered to the public. The choice, again, is not whether moral judgments are made, and so we must take responsibility for these matters.

This is true in politics. When voters are asked to act in politics but then leave their faith to the side, or when elected officials say they will separate out their religious convictions from what they believe to be right, religious judgments are not avoided; rather, these kinds of sentiments themselves represent judgments about the appropriate or desired nature of religious commitment. In this environment, moral decisions are made and enforced without even acknowledging that they are being made, which undermines democratic decision-making rather than enabling it. When we demand that people leave morality and its sources out of our politics, we are condemning them (and therefore our democracy itself) to a life without integrity; we force a division of the soul.

For democracy to be democracy, citizens must be able to be themselves in it, to bring their full selves to it. For Christians to be Christian, there must not be any area of life, including politics, that we cordon off from God, thinking God to be too pure or too inept to have anything to offer there.

But what is it that American Christians have believed their faith offers when it comes to public life? What is their gospel? As we'll discuss in the next chapter, these two questions are more deeply connected than you might imagine.

Chapter 3

GOSPELS OF SIN MANAGEMENT AND OUR POLITICS

When Christians participate in our politics, many Americans do not consider that participation to be good news.[1] There is no single story to explain this—American Christianity is incredibly diverse, and many stories are happening at once—but I believe there is an explanation that makes great sense out of what we see that is both more hopeful and more dire than any of the stories that are commonly discussed. That explanation requires that we first look not at Christians' policy preferences or the maneuverings of politicians but at the popular conception of the gospel in American life—most acutely, perhaps, in American evangelicalism, but also as it influences and has analogs in many other streams of American Christianity.

The disappearance of moral knowledge is not a strictly secular phenomenon imposed on the church. Christians have, wittingly or unwittingly, contributed to it. Christians have bought into it. The primary way this has happened is by the very thing Christians, especially evangelicals, take to be primary—the gospel and their understanding of it.

Here is how Dallas Willard described the problem in one setting:

> We have been through a period when the dominant theology simply had nothing to do with discipleship. It had to do with proper belief, with God seeing to it that individuals didn't go to the bad place, but to the good place. But that developed in such a way that the predominant thought is that a person can have the worst character possible and still get into the good place if he believed the right thing. This disconnection became increasingly burdensome to the church itself until we came to the point that, as is widely discussed, there is not a clear difference between Christians and those who aren't Christians.[2]

Willard describes this as "bar-code faith." This view suggests that "you can have a faith in Christ that brings forgiveness, while in every other respect your life is no different from that of others who have no faith in Christ at all." There's just "something about the Christian that works like the bar code. Some ritual, some belief, or some association with a group affects God the way the bar code affects the scanner."[3] Like a scanner at the grocery store or a retail outlet, it doesn't matter what that bar code is on; the scanner only reads the bar code.

My first job was as a cashier at a grocery store. I applied for the position the day I turned fifteen and worked at the store throughout high school and much of college. The front-end manager would watch a number of metrics to determine which cashiers were effective, but by far the most vital statistic was your RPM (rate per minute), which tracked how many items you were scanning, how many customers you were serving, and how quickly you were helping them. The main thing was that products were moving off the shelf, scanned for payment, and sent on their way "home." Achieving a high RPM is a matter of not just moving quickly but also anticipating where the bar code will be on particular items. The more direct the route you take to scan the bar code, the better your RPM. The best customers were those who would place the bar code facing up on the conveyor belt.

Sometimes, though, a bar code for, say, a bag of green beans would get stuck on a bag of pretzels, and so in the rush of trying to elevate my RPM, I would think I had scanned the bag of pretzels when I had actually scanned the misplaced bar code for green beans. If I didn't notice and the customer didn't notice, that's how we'd close out the order. On to the next customer and the products they had to offer.

Is this how God works? What does it mean to be "saved"? Is being "saved" about having the right label, saying the right words, belonging to the right group? Are the best pastors the ones who know how to get the most people on the conveyor belt, eliciting the right emotional response—bar codes facing up for the Divine Scanner? Does God not notice the difference between a bag of pretzels and green beans? Is God happy for the "green beans" to actually be pretzels as long as they read as "green beans"?

In *The Divine Conspiracy*, Dallas Willard describes and rejects what he calls the "gospels of sin management" on the theological right and the left. I have come to refer to the version on the right as the "fixer gospel."

In movies and television shows about politics and criminal

enterprises, we'll often find a character known as "the Fixer." You can think of The Wolf, Harvey Keitel's character in the movie *Pulp Fiction*, called in to clean up the mess made by Jules and Vincent, played by Samuel L. Jackson and John Travolta. Fixers are brought in to deal with other people's problems. If someone is calling for a fixer, they are typically not just indifferent toward the way their problem is addressed; they actively seek to avoid knowledge of the fixer's work.

The fixer is told by their client, "I don't care how you take care of this, and I don't need to know. Just take care of it." What is important is the arrangement. The fixer is called in to take care of the problem, and then you never want to hear from him again—that is, until the next time you need him. The fixer has no authority or say in the overall operations of the enterprise. The fixer is called in to fix a particular problem so that the enterprise can proceed as planned.

This is a popular view of Jesus in American life and in American evangelicalism. Twentieth-century American evangelism was built around this problem/solution narrative structure, an approach that draws on the lessons of twentieth-century American marketing tactics.

"Why do we need Jesus?"

Well, "we have a sin problem."

Just as you wouldn't need a fixer if there wasn't a dead body and blood on the carpet, the purpose Jesus serves is to answer the sin problem. This is Jesus as "widget." Need to get into heaven? Call Jesus. With that solved, Jesus has served his role and need not speak into much of anything else. The enterprise can proceed as planned.

In the fixer gospel, the essential thing about Jesus and the Christian faith is that he solves the sin problem. How does he solve it? Well, he solves it for those who acknowledge that he solves it. To add anything more to this mental assent would be to add a "work" to the "free gift of grace." Grace, in this view, basically amounts to those instances where God lets you get away with stuff he doesn't need to let you get away with. To say God's grace is unending, that it never runs out, means that God will let you get away with stuff he doesn't need to let you get away with in perpetuity. And it is correct that God does let us get away with quite a bit. It is also incomplete.

"The sensed irrelevance of what God is doing to what makes up our lives is the foundational flaw in the existence of multitudes of professing Christians today," Willard writes regarding the gospel of sin management on the right. "They have been led to believe that God, for some unfathomable reason, just thinks it appropriate to transfer credit from Christ's merit account to ours, and to wipe out our sin debt, upon inspecting our mind and finding that we believe a particular theory of the atonement to be true—even if we trust everything but God in all other matters that concern us."[4]

This may not have been the gospel you have heard, but it does reflect the kind of message—what is presented as essential—that millions and millions of Americans have received and imbibed and promoted. Jesus exists as an answer to the sin problem; he has the golden ticket you need to get to heaven after you die. As long as you have the right answers to a few key questions, you don't have to worry; you're heaven bound.

Willard acknowledges differences among proponents of what I refer to as the fixer gospel (Willard references Charles Ryrie and John MacArthur, among others), but what is shared among them are three basic points: (1) that the issue in salvation is the afterlife—heaven or hell; (2) that "being saved is a forensic or legal condition rather than a vital reality or character . . . the debate then [being] about what must be true of us *before* God will declare us to be in the saved condition"; and (3) that "getting into heaven after death is the sole *target* of divine and human efforts for salvation"—in other words, salvation is not only about life after death; it is the essential reason one would want or seek to be saved.[5]

For people like John MacArthur and Al Mohler, president of the Southern Baptist Theological Seminary, guarding this definition of the gospel is a matter of significant focus. The pursuit of "moral improvement," Mohler has argued, is one of the great "false gospels" out there.[6] Moral improvement alone would, of course, be a false and incomplete gospel, but what is communicated by these warnings about any essential connection between the gospel of a "saving faith" and a person's character is to cast the latter into the realm of the "optional."

Surely the doctrine that it is Jesus Christ who saves is essential. People are not justified by "moral improvement" and cannot achieve salvation "on their own," as Mohler argues—and I agree. We are, as Paul writes in Galatians 2:16, justified by faith in Christ and not by the works of the law. But just as it would reduce the gospel to communicate that it is *only* about improvements in behavior, it is similarly a reduction of the gospel to suggest that Jesus' call is to a series of doctrinal affirmations we make while others head for hell.

These debates may seem overly semantic and removed from topics like politics, but I've come to believe that how people think about the gospel, how they think about God, has much to do with what we see in our politics.

For instance, one's view of the gospel as an arrangement to get into heaven when they die can mean they simply do not think Christianity has anything to offer in politics. Christianity becomes irrelevant or counterproductive to what one's aims should be in politics. The best decision you can make is to give your life to Jesus. However, the fixer gospel is such that people can say that their faith and trust are in Jesus *for their salvation*, yet not trust Jesus at all when it comes to the areas and activities of life as it is lived in the here and now, including politics.

In another report from Tim Alberta at *The Atlantic*, he quotes a "churchgoing attorney" who was considering which Republican he would support for the presidential nomination in 2024. As he talked through his assessment of the options with Alberta, he said, "The Democrats are ruining this country, and being a good Christian isn't going to stop them."[7] This illustrates the point. Where does the churchgoing attorney place his trust?

There is another way in which the kind of thinking behind the fixer gospel finds expression in politics. In 2022, at a political event for the Family Research Council, Albert Mohler said, "We have a responsibility to make certain that Christians understand the stewardship of the vote, which means the discipleship of the vote, which means the urgency of the vote, the treasure of the vote and they need to understand that insofar as they do not vote, or they vote wrongly, they are unfaithful because the vote is a powerful stewardship."[8]

Mohler was criticized for his comments by people who thought it was improper for the head of a seminary to go to a political rally and suggest it would be unfaithful for a Christian to vote in a way that was contrary to his own perspective—which in 2020 was contrary to his approach to the same candidate four years earlier. He defended his comments, tweeting, "If you are offended that I encourage Christians to vote FOR candidates who defend the unborn and support the integrity of marriage and to vote AGAINST candidates who support abortion and subvert marriage, that has been my message for my entire adult life."[9] He went on to refer people to his website.

Indeed, you will find on Mohler's website his "Daily Briefings," which are presented as "a daily analysis of news and events from a Christian worldview."[10] As Mohler's comment would suggest, under the banner of a "Christian worldview," Mohler's briefings focus overwhelmingly on abortion and sexuality. Other than broad topic categories like "politics" and "United States," the topics most frequently covered by Mohler include the "sexual revolution" (tagged 457 times), "abortion" (tagged 283 times), "law and justice" (which is often, though not exclusively, related to abortion, sexuality, and religious freedom—tagged 273 times), and "homosexuality" (tagged 257 times).[11]

In an interview in the run-up to the 2020 presidential election, John MacArthur rejected the idea that there is "Christian liberty" in politics, and after invoking a handful of political issues, he insisted that "no thinking person" could support the political party he opposed. He defined God's priorities for society in a way that was remarkably aligned to the talking points and platform of one of the candidates, priorities that, incredibly, didn't include poverty but did reject "defunding the police."[12]

This fluidity in assessing God's priorities in line with what partisan politics demands is observable with Albert Mohler as well. Prior to the 2016 election, Mohler argued that the national debt is a "monumental moral issue" that amounts to "stealing from future generations." This, too, is a matter of "biblical worldview," according to Mohler, because "the Bible makes very clear, 'Thou shalt not steal.'"[13] This essential biblical worldview issue was not such a priority for Mohler when he was framing the 2020 election, because in that election he was arguing that Christians must vote for an incumbent president who saw the national debt increase roughly 40 percent on his watch.[14]

My point here is not to debate Mohler's and MacArthur's political views, nor to downplay the importance of the issues on which they choose to focus. As for the candidate they supported in 2020, I've consistently stated that I do not believe a vote for Donald Trump was inherently unfaithful, which is not the posture they had toward those who disagreed with them. Furthermore, if they feel called to focus on some issues over others, I have no strictly theological objection to that in and of itself. Thank God that we don't have to try to address every issue under the sun and can rely on others to focus on issues we deem to be important but that we don't feel called or equipped to personally address ourselves.

My objection is to reckless, sweeping charges of unfaithfulness due to the simple fact of voting decisions, which is a common approach in our politics, of which Mohler and MacArthur have been exemplars. They claim God's authority for their prudential judgment about what policies ought to dictate the Christian vote, what positions ought to constitute a biblical worldview. They then hang their judgment around the necks of Christians who are trying to discern their course in politics. One notable facet of these kinds of claims, which are ubiquitous and now shared by politicians and "pastor pundits" alike, is that in the cases of Mohler and MacArthur, they come from people who insist so stridently that we not "add to the gospel" with talk of moral improvement. Their political views and priorities, however, are apparently nonnegotiables of the Christian faith. This kind of politics reflects and is derivative of a strain of American Christianity (not limited to evangelicalism) that offers a political perspective as definitively biblical in a way that reduces Christianity and subordinates it to prudential politics. This has harmed not only our politics, but also the advancement of the gospel.

THE TOOLBOX GOSPEL

It is difficult to come up with a metaphor for the theological left's version of the gospel of sin management. For the theological left, Jesus himself can be treated as a metaphor. The supernatural is stripped out. Whether Jesus was born of a virgin, lived as a boy and later as a man, worked as a carpenter, taught, performed miracles during his public ministry, was sentenced to death, was crucified and buried and resurrected from the grave and is now seated at the right hand of the Father—that any of this actually happened is not essential. What is essential, however, is a number of political and ethical commitments that are read to emerge from the "narrative" of Jesus. If the fixer gospel on the right makes Jesus uncredible by making him irrelevant, this gospel on the left, what I'll call the "toolbox gospel," makes Jesus irrelevant by making him uncredible.

"To be committed to the oppressed, to liberation, or just to 'community' became for many the whole of what is essential to Christian commitment," Dallas Willard explains. "The gospel, or 'good news,' on this view, was that God himself stood behind liberation, equality, and community; that Jesus died to promote them, or at least for lack of them; and that he 'lives on' in all efforts and tendencies favoring them." This was less a theology than a "social ethic that one could share with people who had no reliance on a present God or a living Christ at all."[15]

It's the "toolbox gospel" because Christianity is primarily valued as a source of meaning and power in addressing social and political challenges. It doesn't matter if Christianity is true in any forthright sense of the word, but Christianity is "made true" in the ways people respond to a selection of tools and references to act for social good. Jesus may not have actually risen from the grave on Sunday, but if a riff on resurrection helps to resource continued political action following a defeat, the Christian message then has a purpose.

Jesus and the Christian religion become a means by which certain ethical affiliations are made and pronounced, but you lose "any workable sense in which God and Jesus are *persons*, now alive and accessible, standing in an interactive relationship with those who rely on them."[16] Christianity provides a toolbox for persuasion and motivation for social action, but its power is limited to the emotional response it can provoke, or perhaps its convening and institutional capacity.

Jesus becomes a widget here on the left as he does in the gospel of sin management on the right. God's work in the world becomes synonymous with a political strategy, and Jesus becomes a cheerleader used to stir up emotions for the cause. But when the cause falters or fails to achieve the promised effect, it is Christianity that is judged to be defective. This is when social justice activists burn out or sell out. It's when people running Christian advocacy organizations still use the old language and show up at events in their collars, but no longer actually go to church anymore and spend most of their time critiquing the church rather than building it and serving it.

The political expressions that emerge from the gospel of sin management on the left are not presented as expressions of love, but as love itself. There would be far more accountability for this, far more public blowback akin to what the Religious Right receives, if not for the fact that the public generally does not take the religious content of these expressions seriously in the first place, as they so often, so quickly, become reducible to politics. What other reference point is needed? Faith simply becomes one political constituency of many.

I respect Rev. William Barber II for his efforts to elevate the alleviation of poverty to the center of our politics, but when it comes to specific policies, he has been as willing as Al Mohler to place undue theological weight on his own political analysis. For instance, because it was clear that Democrats would not be able to pass legislation Barber supported through a closely divided Senate, he joined an effort to place pressure on Democrats like Senator Joe Manchin to simply get rid of the filibuster, which allows the minority party in the Senate to block legislation if it cannot receive sixty votes—a supermajority. In a protest in Washington, DC, Rev. Barber did not simply call for Senator Manchin to support getting rid of the filibuster so that Democrats could pass other policies that, in Barber's judgment, would help the poor or protect our democracy; Rev. Barber led the crowd with the slogan, "Filibuster is a sin!"[17]

Now, I know Rev. Barber didn't mean that categorically, because he wasn't shouting that slogan when the Democrats used the filibuster when they were in the minority in the Senate. Surely he would not call it sin to use the filibuster to prevent legislation he opposed from passing the Senate. Perhaps "filibuster is a sin" is shorthand for "filibuster is a sin when it is used to block legislation I believe is vital and just."

One problem with that, and there are many, is that even if someone agreed with all of Rev. Barber's legislative goals, the question of whether getting rid of the filibuster is a good idea is a prudential decision. It could be argued that if you take Rev. Barber's criticisms of his political opponents seriously—they represent the "most egregious forms of extremism"—then extreme caution is required in getting rid of one of the key tools a Democratic minority would have to prevent those opponents from passing the laws they want to pass. Would it be Rev. Barber's "sin" if his advocacy against the filibuster ended up opening the door for laws that harmed the very people he wanted to protect?

The gospel of sin management on the left offers social and political analysis with utter confidence, while the meaning of the Christian faith itself is either reducible to politics or left to the realm of metaphors and symbols, even among those responsible for teaching institutions. Nicholas Kristof's Easter and Christmas columns for the *New York Times* illustrate the point. In these columns, Kristof asks Christian leaders a series of questions, usually beginning with a question about how he admires Jesus' teachings but is skeptical of miracles and claims that Jesus was born of a virgin or resurrected from the grave.[18] Is it okay to take the teachings but leave behind the divine and supernatural?[19]

It wasn't until his 2019 interview with Dr. Serene Jones, president of Union Theological Seminary, that Kristof received the answer he seemed to be looking for.[20] The interview began this way:

Kristof: Happy Easter, Reverend Jones! To start, do you think of Easter as a literal flesh-and-blood resurrection? I have problems with that.

Jones: When you look in the Gospels, the stories are all over the place. There's no resurrection story in Mark, just an empty tomb. Those who claim to know whether or not it happened are kidding themselves. But that empty tomb symbolizes that the ultimate love in our lives cannot be crucified and killed.

For me it's impossible to tell the story of Easter without also telling the story of the cross. The crucifixion is a first-century lynching. It couldn't be more pertinent to our world today.[21]

Pay attention to where confidence is placed. Whether Jesus actually "was crucified under Pontius Pilate, he suffered death and was buried, and rose again on the third day in accordance with the Scriptures," as the Nicene Creed puts it, is uncertain. What is certain is the "symbolism" of the empty tomb, which may or may not refer to an event that actually happened.

This approach continues throughout the interview, as Jones declines to affirm the virgin birth, that God acts on the basis of prayer, or the existence of an afterlife (she suggests there might be "nothing" after we die), but expresses with great confidence the implications of the faith for a range of historical developments and current issues of concern.

What was most interesting about this interview wasn't the answers Kristof received, but his reaction to them. These seemed to be the answers he wanted, yet when he got them, he was quickly dissatisfied. "Isn't a Christianity without a physical resurrection less powerful and awesome? When the message is about love, that's less religion, more philosophy," Kristof responded to Jones's message of symbolic inclusion.

The issue with gospels of sin management on the right and left is not that they are entirely wrong or that they could never be used by God. The forgiveness of sins is utterly essential to Christian living and salvation. We need grace for our sins, even as we need grace for much more. Likewise, Christians should fervently hope that love, God's love, wins the day, and they should certainly seek to address issues of injustice and promote social flourishing. The problem with these gospels of sin management is not that they are right or left; the problem is their "conceptual disconnection from, and practical irrelevance to, the personal integrity of believers. . . . And both lack any essential bearing upon the individual's life as a whole." These gospels "concern sin guilt or structural evils (social sins) and what to do about them. That is all."[22]

While we should be aware of gospels of sin management on both the right and the left, it seems obvious that in recent years, the influence of the right has been far more visceral, identifiable, and consequential. What we've seen unfold has prompted many, including theologically and politically conservative evangelicals, to do some soul-searching and ask difficult questions.

CONNECTING THE DOTS BETWEEN THE FIXER GOSPEL AND OUR POLITICS

I have a friend whom I admire a great deal. I see much of Jesus in him. He cares deeply for the church. He is constantly striving to ground his actions in his faith. He practices humility in profound and tangible ways. He is remarkably transparent.

Still, the last decade or so has left him profoundly disappointed in Christian leadership. He has seen churches torn apart over political disagreement. Christian friends have turned from a lifetime of pursuing faithfulness to choosing political expediency, and pastors have used their influence to excuse the inexcusable. All of this has left him somewhat disenchanted.

He shared with me in an email, "A friend of mine, a person of the Christian faith, recently wrote to me, saying this: 'Christianity is supposed to work—as in produce more

transformed Christlike people. Why doesn't it in case after case?'
People of faith need to grapple openly and honestly with this
question. Potemkin village Christianity serves no one."

My friend continued, "I'm certainly not arguing, then, that
faith isn't making a profound difference in the lives of Christians.
But I do think we need to honestly grapple with the gap between
what followers of Jesus profess and how we live—a gap that will
always exist, but that is right now, at least in America, significantly larger than it should be. What should be a crevice is, in far
too many cases, a canyon."

What we must consider—what Dallas Willard asked us to
consider decades ago—is that the failures of Christians are not in
spite of the gospel that is being preached but because of it. Such
futility is the natural result of gospels of sin management, which
are invitations to take the right positions but are not themselves
Invitations to transformation into the likeness of Christ through
interactive relationship with Christ himself. The kind of person
you are is, at best, a secondary issue for these gospels. Willard
referred to this as the "Great Omission." This "gap between what
followers of Jesus profess and how we live" (as my friend put it in
his email message)—what Willard called the "Great Disparity"—is
rooted in the Great Omission. Though it is not what Jesus taught,
"the governing assumption today, among professing Christians, is
that we can be 'Christians' forever and never become disciples."[23]

To extend Willard's argument, the failures of Christians'
political witness are not coincidental to what Christians have
heard about Christianity and taken it to be; instead, they flow
directly from the plain implications of what they have heard.

We will understand popular expressions of Christianity in
politics and public life much better if we understand the gospel
that is popular among many Christians. If salvation results

from one's mental assent to several lines of doctrine—including, and primarily, that Jesus is the Divine Fixer, the Eschatological Widget—then it should surprise no one that to have a "Christian politics," in some quarters, essentially amounts to mental assent to a few axiomatic political positions.

I have lived and worked at this intersection of faith and politics my entire adult life. It took me so long to connect these dots. What is the popular conception of what it means to be a Christian? A Christian is someone who goes to church, who provides mental assent to a few key lines of doctrine. *What does it mean to have a Christian politics?* For many Christians, and for much of the public, it has meant holding a particular position on one or two key issues. *That's it.* You can advance those positions in the most destructive way possible, through the most deceitful means imaginable, but that would be irrelevant to any decision regarding whether that form of politics was meaningfully Christian. *It's the view of the gospel that allows for and is reflected by the politics.*

If you have a theology that suggests you can be the worst kind of person and make it to heaven as long as you have a moment of mental assent to certain statements, then you can have an approach to politics that is full of anger, fear, and hatred as long as you hold the right positions on a handful of issues. You can go about your politics by deceit, manipulation, and dehumanization and call it Christian, as long as you're willing to say yes when you're expected to say yes, and no when you're expected to say no. The "gospel" and the politics are not disconnected. These things are related. They go together.

Of course, the gospels of sin management are not the gospel, any more than a politics of self-interest and antagonism is a Christian politics.

The right and the left both try to reduce Christianity to an affirmation of their politics. This is not new. People have sought to use Jesus as a vehicle for their politics for a long time; we see it in the Gospels, and we see it today. And yet two thousand years after Jesus lived, died, and was resurrected, his life still saturates our time. The just critiques of Christians are answered entirely by the life and witness of Christ himself.

The gospel of Jesus Christ does not just call in a fixer to dispose of the decaying body and clean the blood off the carpet. It does not merely offer a rhetorical toolbox and inspiration for our political advocacy and social vision.

Jesus is not a fixer; he is Lord. He's not a crisis manager; he is the way and the truth and the life (John 14:6). Righteousness and justice are the foundation of his throne, and he is King (Psalm 89:14).

Chapter 4

KINGDOM POLITICS

A. W. Tozer believed that "what comes into our minds when we think about God is the most important thing about us."[1] One reason for this is that what we think about when we think about God both reflects and colors what we think about everything else, including politics. This is why it was important for us to consider the issues and ideas raised in the previous chapter.

It is also why we now must turn to speaking directly about Jesus. What did he know about God? If we take Tozer's observation seriously, what was the most important thing about Jesus? How might our answer influence and change how we think about and approach politics and how we relate to it?

We can no longer dismiss politics as a distraction from discipleship, evangelism, and spiritual formation. These questions will not simply work themselves out. If Christianity is deemed to be irrelevant to our public life, not only will the public suffer from a lack of Christian resources, but Christian discipleship will have a built-in blind spot—an area in which Christians must act but hold a view of the gospel that actually cordons off Christian resources from guiding their actions.

Nor can we treat Christianity as subservient to politics. It is not safe for Christians to engage in politics with their feet planted in politics. Their political participation must be grounded in a deeper reality; it must be grounded in the gospel.

The principal danger here is not that Christians might end up with the wrong political positions, but that they will have an atrophied faith. Politics must not dictate our thoughts about God. If it does, we will not only do a disservice to the Christian witness, but our faith itself will prove unworthy in the moment of crisis. We must adopt a different way. We must start with Jesus, with his message and his greatest hopes for us—for you and me.

CONSIDER GOD

Jesus' invitation to you is for you to know the world as he knows it and for you to know God the Father as Jesus knows him. Jesus wants you to have a "biblical worldview," but this worldview is not reactionary and it does not have as its principal aim getting you to the "right" political positions. *The kind of biblical world-view Jesus wants you to have is inseparable from the kind of heart Jesus wants you to have.*

To see the world as Jesus sees it is to see the world as it is. It is to peer through tradition, family folklore, and our own messed-up views of who God is and what God must do or be like in order to be God, and see God as revealed in and through the person of Jesus.

Pause here. What do you think of when you think of God? Really. The question is not "What are you supposed to say when you are asked what you think God is like?" Rather, the question is "What do *you* think God is like?" So many Christians believe the Christian life is about filling their heads with the right answers to questions like this, and so they never intentionally come to terms with what they really believe until, in a moment, they act in such a way that they are surprised to learn what they actually believed all along. So what is it that you actually believe about God? What do you believe about the world he made?

Actually, that's a good place to start. Do you really believe that God made the world? What do you think your belief about God and the knowledge that God made the world and everything in it might have to do with one another? Here is what Dallas Willard, informed by Scripture and the life and testimony of Jesus, thought about God:

> We should, to begin with, think that God leads a very interesting life, and that he is full of joy. Undoubtedly he is the most joyous being in the universe. The abundance of his love and generosity is inseparable from his infinite joy. All of the good and beautiful things from which we occasionally drink tiny droplets of soul-exhilarating joy, God continuously experiences in all their breadth and depth and richness.[2]

Can you imagine a joyful God? More to the point, is the God you believe exists the most joyous being in the universe? The reason to consider this question is not so that you can have the right answer or can think of God in a way that is helpful. It is simply a matter of what is real, and if the God of the universe is really joyful, it would likely be a joy for you and me to know it! We just want to know God as he is and live in light of that knowledge.

I once had the opportunity to hear the great jazz pianist

McCoy Tyner play in a small jazz club in Washington, DC. His health was declining—he would pass less than two years after I saw him—and he walked with the assistance of two men on his way to his piano bench. The room was silent as he sat down. His hands ran alongside his pant legs, and his foot adjusted to the pedal. This man played on the two greatest jazz albums of all time—Miles Davis's *Kind of Blue* and *John Coltrane and Johnny Hartman.* Tyner was at that time, arguably, the greatest living jazz legend.

I didn't know what to expect when he began to play, given his health and age, but I was honored to be in the room. His hands approached the keys, and he hit the first chord, which filled the hushed jazz club with such a resounding, harmonious, and beautiful sound that I immediately and unexpectedly began to weep. How was it that I came to be in a room that night to hear such a beautiful, miraculous sound?

I am a sentimental man. I treasure moments like this. Moments of transcendence. Moments of true feeling. The performance of birds chirping as I walk by the creek that runs close to my home; the view from a clearing in the Italian Alps of wildflowers close by and lakes and towns in the distance; an incredible meal prepared and served with care and attention; the evening walk in Washington, DC, when I knew I loved Melissa and the starry night she said yes to my marriage proposal; holding my firstborn for the first time; the heart-stopping smile of my youngest daughter. I revisit these images when I feel distressed or lonely or unsatisfied. I am overwhelmed by the wonders of my lifetime even now as I write this.

"We are enraptured by a well-done movie sequence or by a few bars from an opera or lines from a poem," Willard writes. "We treasure our great experiences for a lifetime, and we may have very few of them. But [God] is simply one great inexhaustible and eternal experience of all that is good and true and beautiful and right. This is what we must think of when we hear theologians and philosophers speak of him as a perfect being. *This is his life.*"[3]

This is exactly right. God is not a perfect being merely because he has perfect ideas about love and peace and joy and justice, but this is how quickly a statement about what is most real becomes clouded by our own assumptions about God and about the gospel. If the gospel is primarily an announcement of the right answers, we easily make God into the perfect exam grader. The idea that God is joyful becomes reduced to a point of trivia, a characteristic worthy of distanced curiosity, similar to the way we might think of Abraham Lincoln's penchant for dry humor or John Adams's affection for his wife, Abigail. Abraham Lincoln's personality might be relevant in some way to our life today, but only inasmuch as knowledge of it might elucidate our understanding of actions he took in the past. It is information. Knowledge about God is not like this. *Knowledge about God's personality is knowledge about life today.*

Read Psalm 145 slowly and take it in:

> I will exalt you, my God the King;
>> I will praise your name for ever and ever.
> Every day I will praise you
>> and extol your name for ever and ever.
>
> Great is the LORD and most worthy of praise;
>> his greatness no one can fathom.
> One generation commends your works to another;
>> they tell of your mighty acts.
> They speak of the glorious splendor of your majesty—
>> and I will meditate on your wonderful works.

Kingdom Politics

They tell of the power of your awesome works—
    and I will proclaim your great deeds.
They celebrate your abundant goodness
    and joyfully sing of your righteousness.

The Lord is gracious and compassionate,
    slow to anger and rich in love.

The Lord is good to all;
    he has compassion on all he has made.
All your works praise you, Lord;
    your faithful people extol you.
They tell of the glory of your kingdom
    and speak of your might,
so that all people may know of your mighty acts
    and the glorious splendor of your kingdom.
Your kingdom is an everlasting kingdom,
    and your dominion endures through all generations.

The Lord is trustworthy in all he promises
    and faithful in all he does.
The Lord upholds all who fall
    and lifts up all who are bowed down.
The eyes of all look to you,
    and you give them their food at the proper time.
You open your hand
    and satisfy the desires of every living thing.

The Lord is righteous in all his ways
    and faithful in all he does.
The Lord is near to all who call on him,

> to all who call on him in truth.
> He fulfills the desires of those who fear him;
> he hears their cry and saves them.
> The LORD watches over all who love him,
> but all the wicked he will destroy.
>
> My mouth will speak in praise of the LORD.
> Let every creature praise his holy name
> for ever and ever.

Do you know that God takes great joy in you? In one talk, Dallas Willard asked his audience to think of a grandparent looking on at their grandchild when contemplating the blessing of Numbers 6:25 that "the LORD make his face shine on you." God looks on you as a mother looks on her baby in its crib. I spent my earliest months of life in foster care, and I don't know how often the people who were entrusted with my care looked on me while I was in my crib. What I do know is that God made his face shine on me, and God has looked on me with compassion and love all of my life. He looks on all of his beloved creation this way—the poor and the destitute, the bumbling and inept, the striving and the complacent, the prideful and the hurried. He looks on you with great compassion and love, even if you look on him with scorn and derision. He sees through all of that. There is nothing you must do for him to look on you this way; he made you.

Christians spend much time teaching that there is nothing one can or must do to earn God's love, but I know many people who are certain they have earned God's hatred. Some reject God's love with the claim of knowledge that God ("if God even exists," they might interject, which betrays an underlying insecurity) certainly has lost all desire for them and could only reject them. Those who think this way place their own limitations on God, but he will not be deterred. It is not that God can't help but love you. God does not love you because he has no other choice. He's not stuck with you. God's love for you is a matter of will—it's what he wants to do.

Willard implores, "We must understand that God does not 'love' us without liking us—through gritted teeth—as 'Christian' love is sometimes thought to do. Rather, out of the eternal freshness of his perpetually self-renewed being, the heavenly Father cherishes the earth and each human being upon it. The fondness, the endearment, the unstintingly affectionate regard of God toward all his creatures is the natural outflow of what he is to the core—which we vainly try to capture with our tired but indispensable old word *love*."[4] As Willard points out, "The miracle is not that God loves me; it would be a miracle if he didn't love me, because he is love. That is God's basic nature—a will to good."[5]

Importantly, God does not love you for who you are pretending to be or what you are striving to achieve. He does not love you for your ideas about yourself. He does not love you for your good deeds. He loves *you*. You do not have to, you cannot, earn it. It is in the light of God's love for us that we are finally freed from the bondage of performance. Practically, *life with Jesus is the only kind of life in which we are free from the need to perform.*

WHAT DO WE SEE IN JESUS?

We see in Jesus the character of God. Jesus told his disciple Philip, "Anyone who has seen me has seen the Father" (John 14:9). Through Jesus, what do we know about the God who created all things, who lives a joyous life and takes great joy in his creation, which he regards with love and compassion?

In Jesus, we see the eternal Word of God made flesh. He lived a life that was like ours in its humanity, and in so doing he showed the glorious potential of humanity. He was faithful to his Father, who was pleased with him. Jesus was a brilliant teacher, the smartest person ever to live, but he was secure, rejecting time and time again the demands that he prove himself or use his intellect to harm others. He was a blessing everywhere he went, meeting people's needs in ways that were obvious and desired by those he met, as well as in ways he knew they needed—even if they did not. He was insulted and abused but never reciprocated. Yet he was no pushover. He lived with the presumption of his Father's love, of his identity and place in the world. He could not be manipulated. Those who felt themselves unworthy simply wanted to get close enough to touch the hem of his garment. Those who were scorned by society received his loving attention. Those who considered themselves authorities encountered him and were left flustered and questioning their own status.

All this and more can be obscured or even disfigured by our own imaginations and presumptions if we are not careful. *If I was Jesus, if I knew what Jesus knew, I would feel . . . I would do . . . I would want . . .*

Three of Jesus' interactions with his disciples help illustrate how our own ideas about *how God must be* miscolor and overcome *who God is* and his actual character and heart for his children.

DID JESUS MOCK HIS DISCIPLES FOR FAILING TO ACT TOUGH?

In the eighth chapter of Matthew's gospel, we're told that while Jesus was teaching, a crowd began to surround him, and so Jesus told his disciples that they would take a boat across the nearby lake. Before they could leave, a teacher approached Jesus and said he would follow Jesus wherever he went. Jesus explained to the man what he was volunteering for—a life on the run. One of Jesus' disciples asked to bury his father before traveling on with Jesus, to which Jesus replied, "Follow me, and let the dead bury their own dead" (Matthew 8:22).

Then, Scripture tells us, Jesus got into a boat and his disciples followed him. "We'd better do what he says," they might have said. "He's been worth following so far."

The passage continues.

> Suddenly a furious storm came up on the lake, so that the waves swept over the boat. But Jesus was sleeping. The disciples went and woke him, saying, "Lord, save us! We're going to drown!"
>
> He replied, "You of little faith, why are you so afraid?" Then he got up and rebuked the winds and the waves, and it was completely calm.
>
> The men were amazed and asked, "What kind of man is this? Even the winds and the waves obey him!" (Matthew 8:24–27)

Dallas Willard suggested in one talk that Jesus reproached his disciples not only for their fear that the boat would sink, but also for "their thought that if their boat were to sink it would be the end of the world."[6] In other words, he reproached them for their overriding fear of danger, of physical harm, of death— fear to the point of the diminishment of their faith. Jesus wasn't castigating them for a failure to perform faith; he was giving them a vision for the kind of security they could find in him that went beyond what they could, at the time, imagine or trust. "Jesus brings the assurance that our universe is *a perfectly safe place for us to be*," Willard wrote.[7] There is evidence in the lives these disciples lived that this was a lesson they remembered, even though they'd have to relearn it again and again.

DID JESUS TAUNT SIMON PETER? (JOHN 21:15–19)

There is a passage in Scripture where Jesus talked with Simon Peter about death. The way a person interprets this passage can be an indicator of what they think about God and the way God views death. Jesus, who had risen from the dead, had joined several of his disciples on the shores of the Sea of Galilee and made them breakfast. After they were fed, he addressed Simon Peter, who had denied that he knew Jesus three times following Jesus' arrest.

> When they had finished eating, Jesus said to Simon Peter, "Simon son of John, do you love me more than these?"
>
> "Yes, Lord," he said, "you know that I love you."
>
> Jesus said, "Feed my lambs."
>
> Again Jesus said, "Simon son of John, do you love me?"
>
> He answered, "Yes, Lord, you know that I love you."
>
> Jesus said, "Take care of my sheep."
>
> The third time he said to him, "Simon son of John, do you love me?"
>
> Peter was hurt because Jesus asked him the third time, "Do you love me?" He said, "Lord, you know all things; you know that I love you."

Jesus said, "Feed my sheep. Very truly I tell you, when you were younger you dressed yourself and went where you wanted; but when you are old you will stretch out your hands, and someone else will dress you and lead you where you do not want to go." Jesus said this to indicate the kind of death by which Peter would glorify God. Then he said to him, "Follow me!" (John 21:15–19)

I'm afraid some of us may read this as a story of Jesus shaming Simon Peter, reminding him of his betrayal and then giving him his punishment. Instead, this is a story of reconciliation, of Jesus assuring Simon Peter of his love. By telling Simon Peter how he will die, he tells Simon Peter that he will be with him, that even in death he will never be abandoned by Jesus. It's a tender moment, not an alpha moment. It's not a punishment; it's an embrace.

Simon Peter's three denials of Jesus (Luke 22:54–62) could be redeemed, made to be a moment of a life that was drawing nearer to Jesus rather than wandering away. It's not a recrimination; it's a commission.

DID JESUS SHAME THOMAS? (JOHN 20:24–29)

These stories have been misused to lay heavy burdens and crushing judgments on people, but Thomas's story is set apart by the fact that he inherited a nickname that would become a byword and a slur against all who would be charged with asking more of Jesus than he could offer or that they deserve. "Don't be a Doubting Thomas," we're chastised. Indeed, if the gospel is a "bar code faith" gospel, the most foolish response to that gospel would be to refuse to just slap on the label of faith and get "checked out" into heaven. *Why couldn't Thomas just say the thing others were saying? Yes, he had doubts—perhaps other disciples did too—but maybe those doubts would just take care of themselves over time. Until then, how foolish would Thomas look if Jesus turned out to be who he said he was?*

The problem with this popular interpretation of the passage is not only that it suggests Thomas is the antithesis of the kind of person Jesus is seeking and approves of, but that it suggests that Jesus is the kind of person who is annoyed by someone like Thomas.

What if we presumed that Jesus looks on Thomas—as Scripture tells us that Jesus looks on us all—with compassion and with love? Look at the account of Thomas's encounter with the risen Jesus anew now, with the presumption that Jesus desires to be known:

Now Thomas (also known as Didymus), one of the Twelve, was not with the disciples when Jesus came. So the other disciples told him, "We have seen the Lord!"

But he said to them, "Unless I see the nail marks in his hands and put my finger where the nails were, and put my hand into his side, I will not believe."

A week later his disciples were in the house again, and Thomas was with them. Though the doors were locked, Jesus came and stood among them and said, "Peace be with you!" Then he said to Thomas, "Put your finger here; see my hands. Reach out your hand and put it into my side. Stop doubting and believe."

Thomas said to him, "My Lord and my God!"

Then Jesus told him, "Because you have seen me, you have believed; blessed are those who have not seen and yet have believed." (John 20:24–29)

Though the text itself, as well as the broader context (directly preceding the story are accounts of others who encountered Jesus directly), said otherwise, for some reason I used to approach this story as if Thomas had seen everything his friends saw, but needed more. Instead, we learn that, unlike some of his friends, Thomas had not had a personal experience with Jesus following Jesus' resurrection. Also, as many commentators have noted, John does not explicitly state that Thomas actually does put his finger where the nails were. It is not the point.

Jesus showed up not to shame, but to serve. As Dallas Willard wrote, "Let's remember that Jesus didn't leave Thomas to suffer without the blessing of faith and confidence; he gave him the evidence he required. That is typical of Jesus's approach to doubt; he responded to honest doubters in the way he knew best, the way that would help them to move from doubt to knowledge."[8]

JESUS' DEATH AND RESURRECTION

If we are to understand who God is, who we are, and God's heart of love for us and the world he made, we must understand not just Jesus' ministry and teachings, but also his death. Again, the intention here is not that we might have more correct answers to a theology quiz regarding atonement and how it works. The aim is that we might live with the knowledge that "God so loved the world that he gave his one and only Son, that whoever believes in him shall not perish but have eternal life" (John 3:16).

This wonderful man, Jesus, who blessed everyone he encountered, who loved and was loved, who wept when he heard of the death of his friend, who was blameless and without sin, died an excruciating death on our behalf so that we might be reconciled to God. The apostle Paul put it this way:

> You see, at just the right time, when we were still powerless, Christ died for the ungodly. Very rarely will anyone die for a righteous person, though for a good person someone might possibly dare to die. But God demonstrates his own love for us in this: While we were still sinners, Christ died for us. (Romans 5:6–8)

Jesus' death demonstrated the extent of God's love for us and the cost Jesus is willing to bear for our good.

Jesus' resurrection demonstrates the power of God's love to overcome evil:

> Who then is the one who condemns? No one. Christ Jesus who died—more than that, who was raised to life—is at the right hand of God and is also interceding for us. Who shall separate us from the love of Christ? Shall trouble or hardship or persecution or famine or nakedness or danger or sword? As it is written:
>
> > "For your sake we face death all day long;
> > we are considered as sheep to be slaughtered."
>
> No, in all these things we are more than conquerors through him who loved us. For I am convinced that neither death nor life, neither angels nor demons, neither the present nor the future, nor any powers, neither height nor depth, nor anything else in all creation, will be able to separate us from the love of God that is in Christ Jesus our Lord. (Romans 8:34–39)

From the life, death, and resurrection of Jesus, we know that God's love for us is not limited by will or power. God loves us, wills our good, and has all the power he needs to advance our good.

He is acting on our behalf now. He is not distant. He is not removed from our circumstances. He is "at the right hand of God and is also interceding for us" (Romans 8:34).

It is not just that we can see God through Jesus, but that God sees us through Jesus. Before he was crucified, Jesus told his disciples that "the Father himself loves you because you have loved me and have believed that I came from God. I came from the Father and entered the world; now I am leaving the world and going back to the Father" (John 16:27–28).

The disciples told Jesus that his words led them to "see that you know all things. . . . This makes us believe that you came from God" (John 16:30).

Jesus responded, "Do you now believe? . . . A time is coming and in fact has come when you will be scattered, each to your own home. You will leave me all alone. Yet I am not alone, for my Father is with me. I have told you these things, so that in me you may have peace. In this world you will have trouble. But take heart! I have overcome the world" (John 16:31–33).

Because Jesus overcame death, we can have his kind of life as our own—right now. And his kind of life holds up in the midst of all this world has to offer.

JESUS IS KING

One of my favorite days on the church calendar is the Feast of Christ the King (also known as the Solemnity of Our Lord Jesus

Christ, King of the Universe). The day was instituted in 1925 as demagogic dictators were taking power in Europe, setting the stage for the Second World War. As secularism rose across Europe and leaders claimed authority separate from Christ, the church reaffirmed that Christ claims lordship over all. In an age when many clamored for power, the church proclaimed the loving authority of Christ. The feast is now celebrated on the final Sunday of Ordinary Time, that is, at the end of the liturgical calendar and right before the beginning of Advent.

Today, King Jesus reigns from the heavens, and he holds all things together. He is victor and safe harbor, healer and champion. He is what was promised in Isaiah 9:6–7:

> For to us a child is born,
>> to us a son is given,
>> and the government will be on his shoulders.
> And he will be called
>> Wonderful Counselor, Mighty God,
>> Everlasting Father, Prince of Peace.
> Of the greatness of his government and peace
>> there will be no end.
> He will reign on David's throne
>> and over his kingdom,
> establishing and upholding it
>> with justice and righteousness
>> from that time on and forever.
> The zeal of the LORD Almighty
>> will accomplish this.

Look past those on the right and left who use the name of Jesus as a pretext for their politics, as fodder for their self-aggrandizement, as cover for their abuse, and look instead to Jesus himself. Over and above the clanging cymbals and the daunting hypocrisy, the hucksters and the sycophants, the false idols and the broken promises, the embarrassed acquiescence of many who know better and the prideful boasts of those who think they know better, Jesus' life remains clear and available to all who earnestly seek him. Jesus is, Dallas Willard wrote, "simply, the brightest spot in the human scene."[9]

What did Jesus want us to most know about himself, about his life, and about what he offers? In *The Divine Conspiracy*, Willard put it this way:

> Jesus came among us to show and teach the life for which we were made. He came very gently, opened access to the governance of God with him, and set afoot a conspiracy of freedom in truth among human beings. Having overcome death he remains among us. By relying on his word and presence we are enabled to reintegrate the little realm that makes up our life into the infinite rule of God. And that is the eternal kind of life. Caught up in his active rule, our deeds become an element in God's eternal history. They are what God and we do together, making us part of his life and him a part of ours.[10]

The good news of Jesus, Willard summarized, is his announcement of the "immediate availability of the kingdom of the heavens to anyone who would simply turn and walk into it. He preached discipleship as the greatest opportunity that any human being will ever have."[11] What is commonly referred to as "eternal salvation"—what happens after you die—is certainly part of the good news, but life with Jesus does not begin when you die. You will find little evidence that Jesus' primary concern in the Gospels is ensuring that people know how to get to heaven after they die. It is *life with Jesus* that is the good news, and that life begins now. As Willard liked to say, "eternity is now in session."

WHAT IS THE KINGDOM OF THE HEAVENS?

What is real? What is reality? Jesus' answer to this enduring question, Dallas Willard tells us, is "God and his kingdom." God is the Alpha and Omega, the Great "I Am." God's kingdom is the *range of his effective will*. Willard explains, "God's own 'kingdom,' or 'rule,' is the range of his effective will, where what he wants done is done. The person of God himself and the action of his will are the organizing principles of his kingdom, but everything that obeys those principles, whether by nature or by choice, is *within* his kingdom."[12]

Willard points to Psalms 145–150 as helpful in presenting God's kingdom to us. We read Psalm 145 earlier in this chapter. This is the "source code" for the kingdom. God's kingdom can be trusted. It is totally good. It will never end. It "has never been in trouble and never will be,"[13] and those who are in it are ultimately safe. Human beings do not produce it, but we can be a part of it.

Where is it? God's kingdom is "not essentially a social or political reality at all. Indeed, the social and political realm, along with the individual heart, is the only place in all of creation where the kingdom of God, or his effective will, is currently permitted to be absent."[14]

Jesus' ministry was about this kingdom, where things happen according to the will of God. He prayed for it and taught us to pray for it: "Your kingdom come, your will be done, on earth as it is in heaven" (Matthew 6:10). Jesus showed us how to live in the kingdom, and he did more than any other person to help us understand its reality. Jesus continues his work of ushering in that kingdom even today, including shepherding us into that kingdom.

We can presume upon the kingdom because it is reliable. Willard once said something that will really help us get to know Jesus and what Jesus has in mind for us: "Jesus is the most presumptuous person that ever lived."[15] That's quite a statement! This passage from John 5, which is representative of Jesus' ministry and approach, exemplifies what Willard meant:

> So, because Jesus was doing these things on the Sabbath, the Jewish leaders began to persecute him. In his defense Jesus said to them, "My Father is always at his work to this very day, and I too am working." For this reason they tried all the more to kill him; not only was he breaking the Sabbath, but he was even calling God his own Father, making himself equal with God.
>
> Jesus gave them this answer: "Very truly I tell you, the Son can do nothing by himself; he can do only what he sees his Father doing, because whatever the Father does the Son also does. For the Father loves the Son and shows him all he does. Yes, and he will show him even greater works than these, so that you will be amazed." (John 5:16–20)

Prior to Jesus' baptism, John the Baptist exhorted those listening to "repent, for the kingdom of heaven has come near" (Matthew 3:2). In the following chapter, after Jesus heard John the Baptist had been imprisoned and Jesus went to Capernaum by the Sea of Galilee in fulfillment of the Scriptures foretelling a Savior, Jesus "began to preach, 'Repent, for the kingdom of heaven has come near'" (Matthew 4:17).

Jesus began his ministry with a pronouncement regarding God's kingdom and its logic by reading from the prophet Isaiah:

> "The Spirit of the Lord is on me,
>> because he has anointed me
>> to proclaim good news to the poor.
> He has sent me to proclaim freedom for the prisoners
>> and recovery of sight for the blind,
> to set the oppressed free,
>> to proclaim the year of the Lord's favor."

> Then he rolled up the scroll, gave it back to the attendant and sat down. The eyes of everyone in the synagogue were fastened on him. He began by saying to them, "Today this scripture is fulfilled in your hearing." (Luke 4:18–21)

The presumption! Jesus really knew something about God, and he acted on that knowledge. This is one reason people reacted to him so strongly and so personally.

THE SERMON ON THE MOUNT

Jesus' teaching in Matthew 5–7, commonly referred to as the Sermon on the Mount, is his most extended recorded teaching on life in the "kingdom of the heavens." For Willard, the kingdom of God and the kingdom of the heavens are not synonymous, particularly as a matter of connotation.[16] Matthew is the only gospel that uses the phrase "kingdom of the heavens" (*basileia ton ouranon* in Greek), and this is because of Matthew's emphasis on the nearness of God as experienced by Israel, a nearness now accessible in a new way through Jesus Christ. The nearness of God—and therefore of his kingdom—is of the utmost importance to Willard and to our understanding of reality. God is close, and the "range of his effective will" is close at hand.[17] It changes everything. He is not constrained to the sky or the clouds, and he's not limited to our "hearts." It is the reign of sin and death that is limited, despite its pretensions, and its trajectory is bending to that of the kingdom of the heavens.

Common readings of the Sermon on the Mount, particularly the Beatitudes, rob it of any practical relevance to life as we actually live it. Instead, the Sermon on the Mount is perhaps the central teaching of Jesus that can inform, to use a popular phrase, "a truly biblical worldview." The Sermon addresses two major questions facing all of humanity: (1) "Which life is the good life?" and (2) "Who is truly a good person?" Jesus' answers to these questions have influenced the course of human history, and their power continues to loom over our lives and our culture.

We will focus here on the Beatitudes:

> "Blessed are the poor in spirit,
>   for theirs is the kingdom of heaven.
> Blessed are those who mourn,
>   for they will be comforted.
> Blessed are the meek,
>   for they will inherit the earth.
> Blessed are those who hunger and thirst for righteousness,
>   for they will be filled.

Blessed are the merciful,

> for they will be shown mercy.

Blessed are the pure in heart,

> for they will see God.

Blessed are the peacemakers,

> for they will be called children of God.

Blessed are those who are persecuted because of

> righteousness,

> for theirs is the kingdom of heaven.

"Blessed are you when people insult you, persecute you and falsely say all kinds of evil against you because of me. Rejoice and be glad, because great is your reward in heaven, for in the same way they persecuted the prophets who were before you." (Matthew 5:3–12)

If the Beatitudes are read as a list of statuses and states to strive toward to receive God's favor, you will profoundly misunderstand Jesus and what he is saying about your life and the reality of the kingdom. Instead, read the Beatitudes in light of Jesus' message of the availability of the kingdom of the heavens.

Willard sets the scene. After healing the sick and attracting huge crowds (Matthew 4), Jesus ascended a hill to teach them. "He does not, as is so often suggested, withdraw from the crowd to give an esoteric discourse of sublime irrelevance to the crying need of those pressing upon him," Willard explains. "Rather, in the *midst* of this mass of raw humanity, and with them hanging on every word—note that it is they who respond at the end of the discourse—Jesus teaches his students or apprentices, along with all who hear, about the meaning of the availability of the heavens."[18]

The Beatitudes do not offer a list of favored classes, a new hierarchy, but a dramatic set of examples—likely, Willard suggests, taken from the crowd before him—of those to whom God's kingdom is available through personal relationship to Jesus.

Jesus is not teaching that it is desirable to be poor in spirit or to mourn, but that "*precisely in spite of and in the midst of their ever so deplorable condition, the rule of the heavens has moved redemptively on and through them by the grace of Jesus Christ.*"[19]

As for the peacemakers, the merciful, and those persecuted because of righteousness, as examples, these are people who operate in ways that often run counter to the world's standards. The merciful, we're told, are suckers. They get taken advantage of and are then blamed for their own victimization. Same for the peacemakers. Instead of picking sides and stoking conflict when it could benefit them, or simply staying out of it, peacemakers have a compulsion to enter into conflict for the purpose of seeing it come to a stable and lasting conclusion. They are naive and fail to appreciate that it's the victors history remembers.

Those persecuted because of righteousness are unable to go with the flow. By their inability or unwillingness to do what it seems everyone else is doing, their conduct is viewed as containing a kind of moral judgment, and in return those persecuted because of righteousness can become despised, even by those closest to them.

I was teaching through *The Divine Conspiracy* with a group of about twenty to thirty individuals, and when we came to Willard's discussion of the Beatitudes, I asked the group to come up with their own set of beatitudes based on their understanding of the kingdom and in light of their experience of life today. Who would you put on the list of those who are blessed in the kingdom of the heavens? Such a list might include the uncultured, the clumsy, the sensitive, the reserved. Willard's modern list includes the "physically repulsive"; "those who smell bad"; the "too big, too little, too loud"; and "the bald, the fat, and the old—for they are all riotously celebrated in the party of Jesus."[20]

When I asked the question in our study group, the last person to answer was Miss Valerie—whom I've come to know as an incredible woman of God. I asked her, "Who would you put on the list of those who are blessed in the kingdom of the heavens?" She answered, "The Squeegee Boys." Miss Valerie lives in Baltimore, Maryland, as do I, and I was overcome at the poignancy of the thought. The Squeegee Boys in Baltimore are primarily Black teenage boys who wash car windows at intersections for compensation. In news reports, the Squeegee Boys are described as objects of pity by some, and as a menace and threat by others. The city of Baltimore has a Squeegee Collaborative, which released a Squeegee Collaborative Working Action Plan. They are, at best, a problem to solve.

Because of the kingdom of the heavens, they are more than that to Miss Valerie, though, and because of her, they are now more than that to me. When Miss Valerie drives through Baltimore and comes to an intersection with the Squeegee Boys waiting, she thinks, *Blessed are the Squeegee Boys.* And now I do too. It's exactly right.

By referencing such a diversity of states and dispositions, Jesus makes clear that life in his kingdom is available to all who earnestly seek it and seek to live according to it. These are the blessed ones, not because they are peacemakers or poor in spirit or meek, but because they have aligned their "kingdoms" with the kingdom of the heavens. The kingdom of the heavens is available to all, including the Squeegee Boys. Including you.

WHAT DOES THIS HAVE TO DO WITH POLITICS?

The story of the blessed Squeegee Boys helps us begin to see what all of this talk of our God-breathed world might have to do with our politics. If you believe we have a mopey God who is counting the ways he's disappointed in you, who regrets that he made you, your belief is going to affect everything about you, including your politics. If God is a joyless scold, wringing his hands about how you've messed up your life, one way to alleviate that crippling sense of judgment might be to find people you think offer a favorable comparison. If God is a cold, distant judge, doling out rewards and punishments based on your productivity and behavior, you might bring that meritocratic view of God's kingdom into your view of how government should operate. You may think:

Yes, I've fallen short, but at least I've never committed a crime. I don't expect God to ever let me off the hook for my sins, so why should the government be anything but merciless toward the misdeeds of others?

I may not be perfect. I held some awful views in my past that I know were sinful, but what that person said is unforgivable! Why do we even allow people like that to vote?

No one helped me get to where I am today. I had to make it on my own. God rewarded me for my hard work and sacrifices, and others should have to do the same.

How we view God has much to do with what we do with the life God has given us.

YOU HAVE A "KINGDOM"

Everyone has a kingdom, and God invites us to be faithful to him with that which is within the range of our effective will. "As a disciple of Jesus I am with him, by choice and by grace, learning from him how to live in the kingdom of God," wrote Dallas Willard. "This is the crucial idea. That means, we recall, how to live within the range of God's effective will, his life flowing through mine."[21]

The eternal kind of life Jesus offers is life with him, learning from him how to live in the kingdom of God now. Such a life is not the burdensome end of a trade in return for which we get access to heaven when we die. It's crucial to understand this. The message received by many according to the fixer gospel is that one can put their faith in Jesus "when they're ready," after they've seen what life has to offer and are ready to "get serious about eternity."

Now, I'm certainly in favor of people putting their faith and trust in Jesus Christ anytime and anywhere, but we must understand that faith and confidence in Jesus are about and for the life we have been given. We are not given a life by God that we are charged to live ourselves as long as we, at some point, check the box of acknowledging that Jesus is Lord so that we will go to the good place when we die. And we are certainly not given a life by God that we are charged to live ourselves as long as we belong to the right tribe and nod yes to the right affirmative creedal statements.

The heavy burden is not following Jesus in this life. The heavy burden is life outside of the kingdom of the heavens. The burden is attempting to manage our lonesome kingdom alone, endlessly seeking to make things happen. "We discover the effectiveness of his rule with us precisely in the details of day-to-day existence," Willard explains.[22]

It is you, the real you—where you live, with your responsibilities, with your experiences—that God wants. And he wants *all* of you. Different Christian communities and streams of thought emphasize different aspects of one's life they ought to think of as particularly "Christian." For some, it's your Sundays that Jesus wants. In others, Jesus is particularly concerned that you have the right sexual ethics or the right views on social justice. In still others, the heart of the Christian faith resides in how you relate to your family or to your nation. But it is *your whole life, as you live it, that is to be lived with God.*

DIRECTLY ADDRESSING POLITICS

In the 1980s and '90s, many evangelical churches, leaders, and institutions came to understand that, for all of the general teaching that was occurring, many lay Christians simply did not see what God had to do with their work life. If asked, they would say that Jesus is Lord, and many would mean it so far as they understood it. It simply had just never occurred to them, as it has never occurred to many who identify as Christian from various denominational backgrounds, what their faith had to do with how they made a living. Such a view is a real problem if Jesus is looking not just for identitarian converts, but rather for disciples. If a Christian does not see what God has to do with their work life, it is likely that there are other areas of their life where they believe that Jesus is irrelevant.

And so, over time, we began to see new institutions spring up around the country like the Center for Faith & Work at Redeemer

Presbyterian Church in New York City. Pastors started teaching sermon series that explicitly connected the general teachings of the faith to their congregants' work rather than assuming they would naturally make the connection. Books were written and practices were developed. The movement hasn't been perfect, but it has made a vital contribution to individual lives, to the church, and to society.

I am convinced that a similar effort is needed when it comes to the Christian faith and public life, including politics—not because politics is the most important area of life, just as work is not the most important, but because the disconnect, the assumption of the irrelevancy of the way of Jesus to politics, is pervasive and apparent. Politics saturates our culture, and so a Christianity that views Jesus as irrelevant to or otherwise not up to the task of our politics, is a Christianity that simply will not be perceived as credible to the public or, I believe, Christians themselves.

FAITH AND POLITICS

As Christians, we must think about politics because politics is within the range of our effective will. It is a discipleship issue.

Christians care about politics because we care about our neighbors and our communities. And political decisions impact the well-being of our neighbors. As a citizen, you do not choose to have political influence; you already have it. Politics is within your kingdom. Therefore, sitting out of politics does not absolve you of blame for the state of our politics; your sitting out is your choice about how to steward the responsibility you have been given.

Faithfulness is not confined to any one sphere of life. While faithfulness may look different in different arenas, it is for *all of life*, including the political. A holistic pursuit of justice and the well-being of our neighbors is inconceivable without political involvement. Politics is one of the essential forums through which we can love our neighbor.

To love our neighbor is to will their good. This is what drives Christians to politics. We don't go to politics to seek affirmation or to find our primary source of identity. Christians go to politics to affirm human dignity and advance justice. Our spiritual and emotional needs are met elsewhere.

Now, our political actions, even those genuinely rooted in love, may not always be received by the public as loving. We remain open to the possibility that our judgments about what prudential action best reflects the "will to good" might be wrong in a particular case or category of cases. This uncertainty is not a blanket license for inaction. To the best of our limited ability, we steward the political influence we have, in reliance on God and with humility and discernment, for the good of our neighbors.

Already, we begin to see how the Christian faith directly provides resources that push back against political hobbyism, political sectarianism, and some of the other ailments we've discussed in earlier chapters. Imagine if we had a politics in which an ever-increasing number of citizens were able to resist and actually push back against the destructive impulses our current politics promotes. Not only would it reduce harm; it would make our politics healthier. Our politics would be freed up, less burdened by people seeking from it what it is not intended to deliver, and we would possess a renewed capacity to affirm human dignity and advance justice in the spirit of love.

We know that political decisions affect the well-being of our neighbors and that the workings of government are essential to the upholding of justice. Love and justice are inextricably linked. As Dallas Willard argued, "Justice without love will *always* fall short of what needs to be done. It will never be as good as it should be. Justice without love will never do justice to justice, nor will 'love' without justice ever do justice to love. Indeed, it will not be love at all; *for love wills the good of what is loved*, and that must include justice where justice is lacking. Justice is a fundamental human good and a prerequisite of many others."[23]

We also see here how Christianity itself contains resources to combat a politicized Christianity that seeks to impose its will through raw political power reforms that would favor particular expressions of Christianity and marginalize all else. This is what has become known as "Christian nationalism," though the term is also now used as a political weapon to critique a whole range of political positions and beliefs in a way I find to be unhelpful and, in some cases, disingenuous. I will not adjudicate that debate now.

What I would suggest is that if you are concerned about the influence of self-identified Christians and Christian organizations that use the faith as a political weapon against others, you should know that it is the Christian faith itself that stands against such abuse. The problem with the political views of many Christian nationalists is not that they are too Christian, but that they are not Christian enough. Their political views fail to uphold the dignity of all people. They fail to will the good of others, including one's enemies.

CHRISTIAN DISCERNMENT AND POLITICS

Here are two things we must remember about politics that pose a challenge to Christians, and specifically to a Christianity of "right answers": (1) politics is prudential, and (2) politics is conditional or contingent. Both of these points are made well by C. S. Lewis:

> Christianity has not, and does not profess to have, a detailed political programme for applying "Do as you would be done by" to a particular society at a particular moment. It could not have. It is meant for all men at all times and the particular programme which suited one place or time would not suit another. And, anyhow, that is not how Christianity works.... It was never intended to replace or supersede the ordinary human arts and sciences: it is rather a director which will set them all to the right jobs, and a source of energy which will give them all new life, if only they will put themselves at its disposal.[24]

So one's political actions are mediated on the front end by this kind of assessment of the various factors and possibilities at play. You may believe, in a vacuum, that a certain policy approach or candidate would be ideal, but *given the circumstances*, the wisest, most loving way forward is a different approach. These kinds of judgments can leave all citizens, Christians or not, feeling conflicted. I would argue that this is good and healthy—but it doesn't mean it's easy.

The difficulties presented by the mediated nature of political involvement loom larger when considered in light of another difficulty of politics—the problem of taking credit. So much of the action we take in service of others prompts a response, sometimes an immediate response, that allows us to know the effect of our action and to take credit for it. Obviously, this is true in the case of helping a close friend or family member. Someone you know needs money or needs help finding a job, and you act to help them. You both know that your action is what made the difference, and you get to see the difference your action made. This is increasingly the case when it comes to charity efforts and institutional involvement. If you donate money to the organization called *charity: water*, for instance, they will send you the GPS coordinates of the well your money supports, and you can watch a live video feed with proof that your contribution is meeting other people's needs.

Politics does not work this way most of the time. Before you take action, you do not know whether your input will make a difference at all. Even after the political act takes place and the process is over, you will likely never know whether your contribution made a difference. In the case of voting, it is extremely unlikely that your single vote will decide an election. The meaning of the vote is not found, oddly enough, in what it accomplishes by itself. Even if the candidate you voted for won, and you want to claim some measure of credit and agency in that outcome, you don't really know what the person you voted for will actually be able to accomplish.

Most other acts of civic engagement don't even offer that much personalized feedback. Was it your letter-writing campaign, your protest, your donation, that pushed things over the top? Or would things have gone exactly the same way if you had never lifted a finger? The mediated nature of politics combined with the uncertain nature of political outcomes can lead to a real and understandable sense of malaise and disinterest.

All of this comes together in the fundamental democratic act of the vote. It is helpful to carefully think through what the vote is and how a Christian ought to consider their vote.

APPLICATION: THE VOTE

The question of voting—particularly as it relates to moral culpability—is one that is very tender and pressing for many.[25] Many Christians feel a moral burden when thinking about politics. Parker Palmer wrote that we have a "politics of the brokenhearted," and Christians ought to have the kind of vision necessary to see that.[26] Politics is causing spiritual harm in this country.

One of the ways it causes harm is by intentionally placing moral pressure, a moral burden, on citizens that fits the interests of political candidates, parties, and activists but does not fit the nature of politics.

To be clear, my argument is not that politics is unimportant. My argument is not that we should not feel any moral pressure when we consider civic action. My argument is that the nature of the moral burden we are so often made to feel—the shape of it—is ill-fitting. It is a burden shaped and cast down in a way that is manipulative. A way that is coercive.

Our political system exacerbates the problem. Because our parties are so polarized and party identity is so profound, we find that politicians and political parties have inordinate influence over the views of the citizenry. We have invested such meaning into what a political party is and what it means to affiliate with one, not because of the nature of a political party, but because of what is in the interest of political parties and other political actors who benefit from them. That is to say: political parties demand our allegiance not because it is their right, but because it is in their interest. We should be members of a political party because we believe things; we should not believe things because we are members of a political party.

In general, political campaigns operate by piecing together a coalition of voters, drawn in by a tailored political platform, outreach, and forms of affinity that will allow them to get to 50 percent of the vote plus one. That is the political mandate of an electoral campaign.

These are the motives of parties and candidates. These are the tools at their disposal for pursuing their objectives. We should be aware of them. This is not to make us cynical but rather to ensure we're all talking the same language.

Political actors, in general, wish to convey that the choice you have as a voter is easy, and they try to raise the moral stakes of making that choice correctly—that is, in their favor. The more easily voters cede their conscience and values to the party or the candidate, the less strain it puts on the party or candidate and the easier their jobs will be. If parties and candidates are brands we identify with rather than a representation of shared deliberation, we can be directed far more easily. What political actors need is our will, and the more malleable our will, the better it is for them.

Here is the thing we must understand: we often think about politics as a forum for self-expression and self-actualization, for the exertion of our personal will, but politics, especially voting, rarely even approaches that because political decisions come to us premediated and multivariable. When we vote in an election, with the exception of a write-in ballot, we are not voting for our dream candidate. Our vote is not an unmediated expression of our identity; instead, our vote is a choice between options we did not choose ourselves. Viewing our vote as an unmediated, pure expression of our will can be debilitating.

Whether or not you are a Christian, to view political choices in such a way threatens the integrity of the human person.

Moreover, for Christians for whom faithfulness is both a means and an end, to view their vote as a totalizing statement of who they are and what they believe inevitably leads to disintegration or quietism, which may be just one path to disintegration.

Because of this, it is a mistake for "pro-democracy" efforts in the United States, including voter registration campaigns, to do what they have done for a very long time—try to motivate people to vote by raising the moral stakes of voting. This marketing strategy runs up against reality because of the very nature of politics. Voting does not feel like we are using our voice in an especially personalized, empowering way. When public relations campaigns communicate to people that it's important to vote or else their voices won't be heard and their values won't be represented, it only amplifies the disconnect many Americans feel between their voice and their vote.

This dynamic is not limited to Christians. At a gathering hosted by Philanthropy for Active Civic Engagement's Faith In/ And Democracy (FIAD) learning initiative, where I have served as an advisor for a number of years, Sabina Mohyuddin of the American Muslim Advisory Council related that in her experience, Muslim clergy were resistant to promoting voting as a panacea because politics was much less clear to them and the vote so much more convoluted than that. I think that this kind of ambivalence is healthy.

Perhaps if we didn't treat politics like one more commercial enterprise that must be branded—like so many product advertisements that saturate our lives—as a way to express our identity or achieve personal status or improvement; perhaps if we treated political life as a limited but vital area of responsibility for citizens that derives its importance not from how it makes us feel but from the dignity of the people who are affected by political decisions; perhaps then we'd see more people who are willing not just to vote but also to participate in politics in an other-centered way.

HOW THEN SHALL YOU VOTE?

We're still left with a basic question: *How should a Christian vote?* If voting is not some pure, unmediated identity statement, what is it? What does faithful Christian voting look like?

Here are some framing questions/concepts to consider when voting:

1. Jesus is not confused about how our politics works. When I talk to some Christians, I get the sense that they think that when they go into the voting booth, close the curtain, and make their decision, they have to exit the booth and explain to Jesus what happened in there. He gets it, I promise you. Politics is not the one area of life that is cordoned off from God.

2. Christians do not go to politics for self-interest alone, but it's okay to consider your own interests, passions, experiences—what God has placed on your heart. We should be transparent about our self-interest, lest we merely play a shell game by conflating our own interest with that of others.

3. We would be wise to listen to others, particularly brothers and sisters in Christ, who disagree with us politically. By consulting others—fellow Christians, experts in our local community, those who are attuned to where the deepest needs are—we seek to vote in a way that is attuned to the time and place we find ourselves in, with particular attention to the poor, the vulnerable, the disinherited, and those who suffer injustice. Our principles are timeless (unless they're wrong, in which case we should change them!); how we apply them will be informed by history, the present moment, and our sense of how God might be moving in the world and in our communities.

Our vote should be directed toward the greatest flourishing of our community. Our vote should be inclined toward the good of our neighbors, as best as we can see it, in consultation with Scripture, Christian tradition, fellow Christians, and our neighbors themselves. We take our vote seriously, but we also recognize we are part of a body politic and we see voting for what it is. And we understand that in all but the rarest of circumstances—and we should be hesitant to suggest in an unequivocal manner what the exceptions are—there is no single Christian way to vote. My principal concern is that Christians vote with *faithfulness* in mind, with *prayer* that intends to expose their heart to God and themselves rather than cover it up, and with a *moral burden* that is rightly sized and rightly situated.

In politics, as in all of life, this means we do not bear the burden of ensuring things turn out right at all costs. Jesus is in control, and he has paid the price. Our call is to be faithful with what we have, leaving the outcomes to him and trusting him. Knowing this, we will begin to view politics as the area of the penultimate and the prudential. Politics is an essential forum in which we live out our love for God and neighbor. Because politics is penultimate, not ultimate, we seek to never allow political ends to come at the cost of faithfulness. We seek to be faithful in politics, but because it is prudential, we understand that it would be a form of blasphemy to flippantly ascribe to our preferred policy instruments and political judgments the weight of religious dogma. The aim is not a political uniformity among Christians but rather a spiritual integrity.

Chapter 5

THE ALLURE OF GENTLENESS: CHRISTIAN POLITICS AS LOVING SERVICE

In *The Allure of Gentleness*, Dallas Willard confronts a real problem. The ministry of apologetics had become "preoccupied with intellectual debates and arguments" conducted, often, "with an arrogant, antagonizing spirit."[1] What was intended to be for the good of others became motivated by a spirit of antagonism toward others. Apologetics, which is fundamentally other-centered, somehow developed into an effort to insulate and protect Christians. "It might help for you to view it this way" turned into "Those people can't even see this!"

I read *The Allure of Gentleness* to apply not only to the work of apologetics but also to Christians' public presence generally, including in politics. *Christians participate in politics not as an act of imposition but out of a spirit of loving service.*

It is this spirit that ought to animate our public activity, Willard argues. "When we do the work of apologetics, we do it as disciples of Jesus—and therefore we are to do it in the manner in which he would do it. This means, above all, that we do it to help people, and especially those who *want* to be helped. That is how all of Jesus' work is characterized in scripture. Apologetics is a helping ministry."[2]

Christian apologetics is "not an attempt to prove we're right." In fact, "the whole idea of defending the faith has become quite a problem."[3] The phrase "defending the faith" comes from Jude 3 ("to contend for the faith"), and it isn't about beating an opponent into intellectual submission or embarrassing someone into silence. Instead, it is about "how you live; it refers to moral purity as well as, no doubt, some elements of correct teaching and right doctrine."[4]

This is an important point to emphasize. It is not that being right is immaterial—it's preferable to being wrong—but we are not saved by our right opinions. The value of being right is that it "enables you to deal effectively with reality and integrate your life with reality appropriately"[5]

Apologetics ought to be done, first, with the "understanding of how valuable and precious people are. . . . One of the things you lose when you engage in defensive argument is your capacity to deal with other people as precious, eternal, valuable souls, persons whom God has . . . a wonderful plan for, for both time and eternity."[6] The second thing we understand is that we're not here to defend the Christian faith; the Christian faith defends us. The third understanding we bring to apologetics is that the primary aim is not to win but to help. If we think the primary aim is to win, we will measure success in a different way than if we think we're in that encounter to help. With the aim to win, Willard once observed, the person in a debate who is successful is the one who makes his opponent shut up. If the conversation includes onlookers, tactics of belittlement or the intention to embarrass can be especially tempting as tools for success. Instead, we are to treat those we encounter with dignity, taking their concerns and doubts and questions seriously.[7]

Do you see how we can apply these ideas to the way we approach politics? Might the idea that we win a debate by making our opponent shut up be relevant in our political life?

We can identify three main aspects of what the Christian's attitude should be when in politics and public life that would powerfully transform the role Christians play in our politics and the way Christians are presented to the public. First, we are to "have confidence in God and God's truth."[8] One popular diagnosis blames Christian confidence for the excesses and failures of Christians' public witness, but this is false. The problem is not that Christians have confidence—and certainly not that they have confidence in God and God's truth. Too many see the strident antics of religious provocateurs, the callous disregard displayed in the public square by some who identify as Christian, and diagnose the problem as Christian entitlement or Christian arrogance. But these frantic performances belie a *lack* of confidence, not an abundance of it. The issue at play is not a people who are made belligerent by their moral confidence but a people whose faith is fragile, whose God is always under threat, always at risk of being made unreal in the event that a political loss occurs.

It is when Christians lose confidence in their security in God's kingdom that they take matters into their own hands. Understand, of course, that confidence is not a synonym for arrogance. And we must be clear in our own minds about exactly where our godly confidence lies. Confidence in God and God's truth, as they are, is necessary and desirable. Confidence in what I think God is or should be doing is dangerous when unmoored from knowledge about God and his world. This is true and apparent in politics. It is our *confidence in God*, who is firmly on his throne, that provides crucial support to both the means we use and the means we do not use in pursuit of political goals. We'll return to this idea later in this chapter.

Second, we are to be "humble, generous, and open."[9] This is Willard's advice when it comes to Christian apologetics, discussions about ultimate things. How much more important must this be, then, when we are talking about *penultimate* things! Empowered by our rightly placed hope and confidence in God's kingdom, Christians can be a nonanxious, nonmanipulative presence in politics and public life. This is not an aloofness, but rather a generous engagement. We hold our political views with open hands. We have real knowledge to bring, which we bring with confidence, but part of that knowledge is the contingent nature of our politics and the precarious nature of the development and enactment of public policy.

Finally, we are to have a "true desire to lovingly serve."[10] In a spirit of reflection, Christians will ask God to search their hearts as to whether their public presence is motivated by and truly reflects loving service. Confidence in God's kingdom leads us to seek the good for others through our political involvement. "Love means that we humbly and simply devote ourselves under God to the promotion of the goods of human life that come under our influence. We live to serve," Willard writes.[11]

After he rejects conceptions of religious pluralism that require an absence of conviction or require that Christians pretend not to know what they know, Willard argues this:

> Yet there is something right about pluralism, once we get
> past these "impossible" understandings of it, and it clearly
> has to do with how we treat those who disagree with us on

religious matters, and especially with how we treat other religions and their practitioners. It has to do with having a proper attitude toward them, treating them well, and being appropriately modest and nondogmatic about our own views. If we do know something, that does not mean we are infallible and could not be wrong about it. In explicitly Christian terms "pluralism" has to do with accepting those we don't agree with as our "neighbors" and loving them as we love ourselves— with treating them as we would like to be treated if we were in their place. This distinctively Christian imperative is precisely based upon the knowledge of God, Christ, and right and wrong that we claim as Christ followers. It concerns respect for the sincere efforts of human being to do what they believe to be good and right.[12]

In this paragraph, Willard applies to our diverse society the confidence, generosity, openness, humility, and spirit of loving service he recommends in *The Allure of Gentleness*. This kind of approach is not a calculated strategy for success. Willard is not suggesting that you "try to appear humble, which might get you what you want." No, what we want is to be like Jesus, and Jesus taught us that he came among us as one who serves (Luke 22:27) and that to be great means we will look to serve others (Matthew 20:26).

WHAT CAN STAND IN THE WAY OF A KINDER, GENTLER POLITICS?

In order to move beyond thinking that a politics of loving service is merely a nice idea, we must confront directly the real and perceived obstacles to such an approach. People give at least five reasons to explain why a more loving politics is not possible or even advisable.

1. We Need Anger

First, gentleness is rejected in politics because people believe the cultivation of anger is both useful and inescapable. In political philosophy, it can be viewed as enlightened, even idealistic, for politics to serve as a forum for playing out our hatreds. Politics, the philosopher Michel Foucault argued, is "war by other means."[13] So long as people are processing their anger through politics, the thinking goes, they are less likely to express it through violence. Of course, from military action to capital punishment—and all of the other ways political decisions can directly or indirectly lead to violence—we should be careful to discern how much violence our politics avoids versus how much it redirects. Still, it might be argued, politics makes anger respectable.

Moreover, it is thought that anger is a natural response to injustice, and without it, the redress of injustice will never take place. Now, there is a critical way in which this is true. As Dallas Willard wrote, "In its simplest form, anger is a spontaneous response that has a vital function in life. As such, it is not wrong. It is a *feeling* that seizes us in our body and immediately impels us toward interfering with, and possibly even harming, those who have thwarted our will and interfered with our life."[14] Anger plays an indispensable role in human affairs.

In politics, anger can rise up in response to a specific action that is taken or an experience that has been endured as a result of the functioning of government or the consequences of political action. This, too, is legitimate. We would almost certainly do more harm than good were we to, as a matter of social sanction, penalize or seek to limit the feeling of anger arising among individuals in a community. We might, though, seek to become the kind of people who react to a variety of circumstances, including political circumstances, with an immediate response that differs from anger. Still, for the sake of our present discussion, let's put aside the immediate emotional response of anger as a result of interference with our will, and especially injustice. Here we are focused primarily on cultivated or nurtured anger.

We must recognize several things about anger and our politics. First, all of the anger in our politics does not derive from politics itself. Much of that anger is of a personal nature, deriving from circumstances and infractions that are not fundamentally caused by political decisions. With the encouragement and effort of political powers, people bring their anger (as well as their fears, resentments, affinities, and so forth) to politics, with a desire to process those feelings through our politics itself. They are encouraged to do this. One reason is that the greater someone invests those emotions that grip them into our politics, the greater our politics and political interests will grip them in return.

Not only is much of the anger in our politics not caused by or likely to be resolved by politics, but our political system intentionally and methodically cultivates anger. Political activists, academics, and politicians testify to the *usefulness* of anger in our politics. Studies have shown anger can motivate political behavior,[15] and the scientific ratification of that fact lends all the sanction that many people who have power need, in response, to stoke anger.

As we discussed in an earlier chapter, this is an openly declared strategy. Journalists and pundits grade politicians' effectiveness and prospects by how well they are able to tap into voters' anger. Strategists consider how anger might be cultivated and channeled to their benefit. Advocates, including Christians, not only praise the utility of anger but charge that *to not be angry is worthy of condemnation.* "If you're not angry, you're not paying attention," the saying goes.

Now, I am convinced that anger is of some utility to political actors. I've seen it up close. Your anger is very useful to others. Affirm someone who is angry, and you'll find you have influence with them, even if they may not have influence with you. This is part of the nature of anger. It is easily manipulated. It's not difficult for actions motivated by a cultivated anger to become detached from any practical redress of the source of anger in the first place. We begin to nurture and cultivate anger only to find that anger is cultivating us, changing us. As Augustine observed, "Hatred of another insidiously creeps upon us, while no one who is angry considers his anger to be unjust. For anger habitually cherished against anyone becomes hatred, since the sweetness which is mingled with what appears to be righteous anger makes us detain it longer than we ought in the vessel, until the whole is soured, and the vessel itself is spoiled."[16]

It is this cultivation of anger that we must recognize as deadly. "Anger first arises spontaneously," Dallas Willard wrote. "But we can actively receive it and decide to indulge it, and we usually do. We may even become an angry person."[17] As Howard Thurman recognized, anger has an incredible creative capacity.[18] People find that anger can be a source of motivation in their life. And cultivated anger always produces a cover of self-righteousness.

Contempt is worse than anger. "Unlike innocent anger, at least," writes Willard, "it is a kind of studied degradation of another."[19] Contempt is inherently dignity-denying, unlike anger. There is anger in our politics which does not necessarily degrade the basic worth of others, but contempt has the intent to "exclude someone, push them away, leave them out and isolated."[20] A politics of contempt promotes social conflict, isolation, and a lack of belonging, though that can be difficult to see if we view the practice of politics as a game that is neatly separated from the kind of people we are. Anger and contempt become promoted as necessary tools in political warfare.

Some of the worst behavior in our politics is wrongly rationalized by the patronizing notion that this behavior represents the unfiltered cries of those who suffer, who have been ignored, or who feel the most neglected, and that to critique the culture of our politics is a form of "respectability" that can only create barriers of entry to our politics.

As long as the political positions are correct, as long as the political expression supports the "right side," almost anything can be excused or explained away. If one's political opponents express themselves through the use of insults, mockery, vulgarity, or contempt, it becomes more evidence against them and their policies. Yet if these same kinds of expressions come from one's own side, they become raw expressions of truth, the "cry of the people." Some even argue that these kinds of expressions are necessary for a truly democratic politics. Contempt becomes the marker of authenticity.[21]

The fatal philosophical flaw here is with the notion that one's character is fundamentally a result of one's circumstances and experiences. This idea dishonors human dignity, and a full commitment to formation, to character, cannot take place if it is embraced.

What won't surprise anyone who has spent time with people

of various education and income levels is that these markers don't get you very far when it comes to determining the quality or character of a person. This truth extends to consideration of the kind of person someone is when it comes to politics.

But this is how it works. We find justifiable cause for anger, envy others' anger and the supposed freedom and authenticity that come with it (in reality, it is bondage), and cultivate and add to the justifications for our own anger. As we discussed earlier regarding political sectarianism—and the aversion, othering, and misplaced moralization that upholds it—this downward spiral of reciprocated anger is evident in "a nation increasingly sick with rage and resentment of citizen toward citizen," as Willard himself observed. "The sense of self-righteousness that comes with our anger simply provokes more anger and self-righteousness on the other side."[22]

Augustine advises that "it is incomparably more for our soul's welfare to shut the recesses of the heart against anger, even when it knocks with a just claim for admission, than to admit that which it will be most difficult to expel, and which will rapidly grow from a mere sapling to a strong tree. Anger dares to increase with boldness more suddenly than men suppose, for it does not blush in the dark, when the sun has gone down upon it."[23] While our culture bends toward affirming anger, Augustine advises that our disposition should be to resist, for the sake of our souls, the temptation of cultivating even anger that stems from true and direct wrong against us.

This is no reason to downplay social injustice. In fact, the inclination to downplay it, to ignore it, should be rejected by Christians, not just for its material harms, but because we understand what it does to individuals' souls. We know that injustice provokes the natural response of anger, and with repeated injustice the ever-growing temptation to give oneself over to anger. In this way, appeals by Christians to ignore injustice or politics in favor of "saving souls" are undone, refuted by the very knowledge contained in the Christian tradition.

Christians take injustice *more* seriously because we are not mere materialists. We believe there is more to the human condition than our physical well-being. We understand that human beings have souls, and we care for the whole person. Unjust systems and conditions that tempt people to anger and despair are, for this reason, more evil, not less, than secular activists claim.

Put aside what so many politicians and activists promote, what so many say you need, and consider whether Dallas Willard might be right: "There is nothing that can be done with anger that cannot be done better without it."[24]

2. We Need Fear

The second obstacle to a more loving politics rises from the fact that our political system thrives off of and seeks to cultivate fear. Our response to the fear held by specific individuals in our politics, like our response to anger, should rarely, if ever, be to dismiss it or belittle it. Still, like anger, fear is promoted and used by political forces, and fear is used as justification to do harm to others. That which causes us to fear, like that which provokes us to anger, may or may not be real. Dallas Willard believed that life in God's kingdom made fear unnecessary, though no one should feel guilty for being fearful.

Now that you've read that, you are likely already coming up with a list of things that make you fearful, that seem, well, scary. Consider whether a state of fear is contributing to your life in a positive way and whether you might be better off without it. Reflect on Psalm 23 and Romans 8, and put the object of your fear in the light of those statements of reality about God's kingdom. We can grow in this area, even to the elimination of fear as a force in our life and decision-making.

Even if we cannot conceive of life without fear, we must come to terms with how fear is used to promote and justify an antisocial politics that, if embraced, precludes gentleness. *The invocation of fear as a reason that gentleness in politics is unrealistic ultimately lends itself to finding one's security in politics.* If circumstances can lead us to sacrifice gentleness in pursuit of a political outcome, it is likely because we fear not getting something from politics that we believe we need more than what God will provide if we are faithful. This fear paves the way for a downward spiral of rationalizations.

Some attempt to obscure this shifting of loyalties by depicting their fear, and promotion of fear, as a defense of Christian values—a wildly effective move in recent American history. *I worry about a church that fears the power of cultural and political circumstances more than it fears the power of God.* It is where we seek refuge when we fear a potential outcome that indicates where we put our trust and find our security.

We may harbor doubts about whether we can live without fear, and we should take those doubts to God. But let us harbor no doubt about whether God requires our fear. He does not. "Jesus . . . brings us into a world without fear. In his world, astonishingly, there is nothing evil we must do in order to thrive."[25] For Christians, fear is no justification to affirm conduct or a spirit in politics that is not of Christ.

Indeed, to those who insist we need fear and anger to pursue justice, I suggest they observe that wherever injustice is, fear and anger are almost certain to accompany it. It is injustice that requires fear and anger, not justice.

One final note regarding anger and fear in politics. It must be acknowledged that anger and fear are promoted through increasingly sophisticated systems and campaigns. People are led to fear things they never would have thought to fear, and to be angry about things they never would have thought to be angry about, because such a stance is deemed to be in service of a political cause. To reject fear and anger in our politics should mean not only that we take steps to guard ourselves against this manipulation, but that we oppose the manipulation itself. We do this because we know that fear and anger corrode souls and harm social relations. We do this because we are taught not to fear and to be slow to anger, and a politics that promotes fear and anger runs counter to what is best for the human spirit. We reject anger and fear, but we offer compassion and understanding for those who are angry and afraid. What is most worthy of scorn is the cultivation of fear and anger from a place of security, the political merchants who artificially promote fear and anger for self-gain and the manipulation of others.

3. We Need Vulgarity

The third objection to a gentler, more loving politics is that politics is viewed as a forum for self-expression and self-affirmation. In our politics of personality, it seems to some that our politics would be disingenuous if our politics was *not* a reservoir and stage for our most unfiltered expressions. Along these lines, some have decided it is a problem that our politics is not more vulgar. Vulgarity is the language of the people, and a politics that does not speak in that language is not properly representative. Here's how one writer on the political left put it: "Reclaiming vulgarity from the Trumps of the world is imperative because if we do not embrace the profane now and again, we will find ourselves handicapped by our own civility. Vulgarity is the language of the people, and so it should be among the grammars of the left, just as it has been historically, to wield righteously against the corrupt and the powerful."[26]

Yet to the extent that vulgarity is indeed the "language of the people," we ought to decide as the people that we do not want or need to bring that language to our politics. This applies to our public conduct more broadly. Our public life does not have to be and should not be the unmediated expression of our every thought and feeling. Some thoughts, feelings, and ideas are not inherently political. They have no real relevance to self-government, and we should not ask our politics to process those things or respond when politicians or other political actors seek to use those things for their purposes. Other thoughts, feelings, and ideas are political but destructive, and we must consider whether those thoughts, feelings, and ideas can be brought to our politics in a spirit of loving service. If not, we should restrain ourselves and assess the source of those thoughts, feelings, and ideas and how we might submit them to the Lord.

4. We Need Certainty

Fourth, because politics is viewed as a profound, unmediated expression of one's personal identity and values, many who feel conflicted or uncertain about politics believe their posture disqualifies them from political participation. It seems best, in numerous ways, to leave politics to those who at least appear to be certain. This way of thinking results in indifferent detachment until, importantly, a political development occurs that they believe finally offers the clarity to justify their involvement. Then the formerly indifferent and detached are capable of great levels of belligerence, for they have no positive vision of politics.[27]

The conception of what they once rejected in our politics is now just one they have embraced as they give themselves over to the fear and anger that once kept them away from politics.[28]

5. We Need Antagonism

The fifth objection has to do with confusion around pluralism and a belief that a loving, gentle politics simply is not viable in a largely antagonistic political and cultural environment. We are warned that if we go about "loving our enemies" in *this* culture at *this* time, we'll be steamrolled. This argument is pervasive today, and it has been readily embraced by many Christians.

The response of some Christian leaders who have identified the political damage and spiritual temptation of thinking that the times require using the tools of the enemy (note the similarities of this argument to that of the leftist writer above regarding vulgarity; both use characterizations of "the other side" to justify their actions and recommendations) has been to argue that things are not really that bad. Now, surely they are right in the sense that the depictions of the culture used to justify unchristian behavior are exaggerated, incomplete, and myopic. However, I think it's clear that twenty-first-century America relates to Christianity differently and, in certain ways, more antagonistically than it did in the previous century. Recall our discussion of the disappearance of moral knowledge in chapter 2. The implication of focusing on the current culture is that it suggests that the viability of Christian conduct rests on the culture. Instead, we must reject a loving politics as a strategy and embrace it as a commitment. Even if we do find ourselves living in Babylon, let's be sure we don't find ourselves becoming Babylonians.

WHERE JESUS STANDS IN OUR POLITICS

Christians act in politics and in all of life in light of what we know about God and the world he has made. Why wouldn't we? It is in God that we live and move and have our being (Acts 17:28).

One aspect of how we relate to God's kingdom that Dallas Willard thought was crucial was discussed by Dietrich Bonhoeffer in his book *Life Together*. If Christians truly considered this idea and took it with them into politics, our public life would be transformed.

As Christians, when we encounter another person, we do not seek to love them directly. We do not bring with us "human love" alone, but God's love as well. Bonhoeffer explains, "Human love has little regard for truth. It makes the truth relative, since nothing, not even the truth, must become between it and the beloved person.[29] Human love desires the other person, his company, his answering love, but it does not serve him. On the contrary, it continues to desire even when it seems to be serving."[30]

Human love is, by its nature, "desire for human community." Where human love can satisfy this desire, "it will not give it up, even for the sake of truth." However, when it becomes clear that human love will not be reciprocated, that the desire for human community will not be met, "it stops short—namely, in the face of an enemy. There it turns to hatred, contempt, and calumny."[31] *Human love alone will fall short in politics at the very point at which it is needed, at the very point that it stops working as a strategy.*

"Human love makes itself an end in itself. . . . It loves itself, and nothing else in the world," Bonhoeffer continues. "Spiritual love, however, comes from Jesus Christ, it serves him alone; it knows that it has no immediate access to other persons.

Jesus Christ stands between the lover and the others he loves."[32] Reflecting on Bonhoeffer's insight, Dallas Willard tells us that Christians never meet one-on-one: "I never think simply of what I am going to do with you, to you, or for you. I think of what we, Jesus and I, are going to do with you, to you, and for you."[33]

As Bonhoeffer wrote, "Because spiritual love does not desire, but rather serves, it loves an enemy as a brother. It originates neither in the brother nor in the enemy but in Christ and his Word. Human love can never understand spiritual love, for spiritual love is from above; it is something completely strange, new, and incomprehensible to all earthly love."[34]

Whereas human love has the instinct to dominate and coerce, spiritual love requires that we meet another "only as the person that he already is in Christ's eyes. . . . Spiritual love recognizes the true image of the other person which he has received from Jesus Christ."[35]

"Therefore, spiritual love proves itself in that everything it says and does commends Christ. It will not seek to move others by all too personal, direct influence, by impure interference in the life of another. . . . This spiritual love will speak to Christ about a brother more than to a brother about Christ."[36]

This is our God-breathed world. This is the life that God has given to us, which he invites us into. This is his kingdom. It is so much more than the promise of life after death, though it includes that. It is so much more than inspiration for a commitment to love and social justice, though it includes that as well. *God is present in our midst. He stands between us and our fellow citizens, and he wants us to see them as he sees them.* Such sight, such love, is no guarantor of political success. It is no guarantor of reciprocation. But it is the kingdom way. It is where we live.

Gentleness is viable in our public life. So are joy, peace, forbearance, kindness, self-control, goodness, and love. But our public presence, our posture toward and in politics, will not reliably and consistently reflect the fruit of the Spirit without effort on our part in reliance on God. As we walk farther down this path, we come to a concentrated focus on the central question of this book: How do we become the kind of people our politics needs?

Chapter 6

THE KIND OF PEOPLE WE ARE

We live in a world filled with the glory of the knowledge of the Lord and all that he has made. We are created beings in a created world that God proclaimed good. He has pursued the good for his creation from the very beginning. Even in the face of death and disappointment and evil, God advances his will through people who seek him. This is the story of Abraham, Esther, Job, Daniel, and David. It is the testimony of the saints, and it is the story of women and men you know—people who would say that without Jesus, the person they used to be never would have done the things they do now and never could have been the person they are today. They are the people who know that "with God all things are possible" (Matthew 19:26) because they are being renewed in knowledge in the image of their Creator (Colossians 3:10).

In his ministry, Jesus announced the ever-present availability of the kingdom of the heavens, a kingdom that surrounds us, and taught us to pray that our Father's will be done in all areas of life as it is done in the heavens. Through faith and confidence in Jesus, we are learning how to put our kingdom, that which is under our effective will, under God's kingdom. We are learning to seek God's good and the good of our neighbors wherever we are and in whatever we do. We are becoming the kind of people who can do so naturally out of the overflow of our hearts.

It is in and through this vision of the reality of God's kingdom and our life in it that we see politics because we have responsibilities under our effective will that pertain to politics. Moreover, politics is an area of life explicitly charged with duties of service to others and stewardship—an area of life with significant influence over the well-being of our neighbors, particularly the poor—and we care a great deal about the well-being of our neighbors. God, who is love, wills the good of all who come into contact with his kingdom. As we grow into Christlikeness, so will we.

What matters most to God is the kind of people we are becoming. Not what we produce. Not the positions we hold. Not the status or reputation we've acquired. What kind of persons are we?

This chapter will consider how we become the kind of person our politics needs.

We can summarize some of the knowledge we've gained about politics:

1. Politics is *prudential.* It rarely, if ever, allows for the direct implementation of indisputable principles, but rather has to do with an imperfect choosing between competing values and goals.

2. Politics is *contingent.* The propriety of a political decision relies in part on the particular circumstances of the moment in which it is made. A wise political decision in one time and set of circumstances will likely be foolish in another.

3. Politics is *important, but not ultimate*. Politics is penultimate, which means that politics can be informed by the ultimate but is never the ultimate itself.
4. Politics is for *advancing justice* and *affirming human dignity* as it relates to (self-) government.
5. Politics is an essential forum for *loving your neighbor*, for *willing (or intending) their good*.
6. Much political action, especially voting, is *mediated by structures and community*, not simply a pure expression of one's personal desires or preferences.

This knowledge must inform what we are about to consider, which is what it means to be the kind of person our politics needs. Critically, this requires that we discuss spiritual formation.

WHAT IS SPIRITUAL FORMATION?

Spiritual formation is not a question for Christians alone. It is not optional, something that *may* come up in one's life. While it has a particular connotation today, spirituality is not a matter of a certain kind of aesthetic or set of preferences. The phrase "I am a spiritual person" is redundant. Every person is spiritual because every person has a spirit. Likewise, every person has undergone a process of spiritual formation.

"Spiritual formation," Dallas Willard wrote, "without regard to any specifically religious context or tradition, is the *process* by which the human spirit or will is given a definite 'form' or character. It is a process that happens to everyone. . . . We each become a certain kind of person in the depths of our being, gaining a specific type of character."[1]

If spiritual formation is so central to the human experience, why is it viewed as a niche interest, even within the church? There is a great deal of talk now of identity and self-discovery. Our culture is full of references to self-improvement, especially in terms of developing a person's skills, appearance, or achievements. Spiritual formation is about *something deeper.*

The reluctance to focus on spiritual formation as a matter of public import certainly has something to do with the disappearance of moral knowledge, as well as a cultural discomfort with the idea that anything can be *known* about what makes a person good. Interestingly, we rarely cease to make judgments about what makes for a good life—the desirability of certain jobs, relational milestones, appearances, cultural tastes, and so forth—but we are hesitant to make judgments, especially public ones, regarding what makes for a good person.

While spiritual formation is about the "inner life," public life is about what is external, or so the thinking goes. We delude ourselves into thinking that what *really* matters in our public life is not one's thoughts, feelings, and intentions, but one's conduct and output. One might even quote Rev. Martin Luther King Jr.'s declaration that "it may be true that the law cannot change the heart but it can restrain the heartless. It may be true that the law cannot make a man love me but it can keep him from lynching me and I think that is pretty important, also."[2] Some use this quote to suggest that the thing the law *can* do is the most important thing that could be done. This is not King's meaning. In fact, he is affirming the penultimacy of government, the inadequacy of politics to fully address the greatest human needs.

Preceding the passage quoted above, King says, "Now the other myth that gets around is the idea that legislation cannot really solve the problem and that it has no great role to play in this period of social change because you've got to change the heart and you can't change the heart through legislation. You can't legislate morals. The job must be done through education and religion. Well, there's half-truth involved here. Certainly, if the problem is to be solved then in the final sense, hearts must be changed. Religion and education must play a great role in changing the heart."[3]

It is not that it is better to restrain the heartless than to change the heart, but that it is directly within the power and responsibility of government to seek to restrain the heartless, while it is not within its power to determine and transform the nature of one's heart. Indeed, government cannot even reliably thwart the will of the heartless. While government can criminalize whatever it wants, its ability to enforce those laws and prevent infractions against them is limited.

Again, this is not to unduly diminish government and the effects of good laws. Speeding laws have not ended all speeding, and people often speed and face no consequence, but that does not negate the accidents that have been prevented—and lives that have been saved—by those laws.

As a parent, I might as a matter of convenience or necessity tell my children before an outing that they will receive some benefit if they do not fight with one another during the outing. This might address my immediate need and avoid a worse outcome in the short term, but it is costly. More importantly, it does not achieve what I am really after. I know as a parent that even if a fight is avoided, the need to provide an incentive to achieve that outcome is an indication of deeper dysfunction— dysfunction that all of my planning and systems may not be able to restrain for the rest of the evening, not to mention the next week or month or year.

What I'm really after as a parent, of course, is to help my daughters become the kind of people who would never even think of fighting with one another. I want them to be so full of love for each other, so other-regarding in the way they relate to one another, that they would be indifferent to, perhaps even insulted by, the suggestion that they are merely an ice-cream cone away from doing each other harm.

The problem King is addressing, at its root, is not lynching, but rather the fact that individuals in his society were the kind of people who could, under certain circumstances, desire to inflict harm on Black people with such intention that it reliably resulted in actions such as lynchings as well as an unimaginable panoply of other actions and behavior meant to harm Black people. Government is incapable of full redress for those harms, and the fact that government has not yet redressed that which it is capable of redressing is yet another indication of the centrality of the heart in these matters.

It is folly to think of advancing the "Christian worldview" in politics separate and apart from advancing in formation into Christlikeness. This has been the fatal flaw at the heart of so many Christian advocacy organizations, worldview movements, political campaigns, city ministries, and strategies for influence. Too often, strategies aimed at political and cultural influence amount to efforts to clean the outside of the cup in the hope that the inside will somehow get clean as a result.

C. S. Lewis explains it well:

> A Christian society is not going to arrive until most of us really want it: and we are not going to want it until we become fully Christian. I may repeat "Do as you would be done by" till I am black in the face, but I cannot really carry it out till I love

my neighbour as myself: and I cannot learn to love my neighbour as myself till I learn to love God: and I cannot learn to love God except by learning to obey Him. And so, as I warned you, we are driven on to something more inward—driven on from social matters to religious matters.[4]

Dallas Willard affirms the basic point, citing T. S. Eliot, who once described the current human endeavor as "that of finding a system of order so perfect that we will not have to be good." Willard continues, "The way of Jesus tells us, by contrast, that any number of systems—not all, to be sure—will work well if we are genuinely good. And we are then free to seek the better and the best."[5]

How, then, do we become good?

CHRISTIAN SPIRITUAL FORMATION

Christian spiritual formation is the "Spirit-driven *process* of forming the inner world of the human self in such a way that it becomes like the inner being of Christ himself."[6] Christian spiritual formation is "focused entirely on Jesus. Its goal is an obedience or conformity to Christ that arises out of an inner transformation accomplished through purposive interaction with the grace of God in Christ."[7]

It is not mere behavior modification, though the behavior of someone who has progressed in Christian spiritual formation will certainly be different from what would have been their behavior prior to such progression. The aim is not a particular presentation or a veneer of respectability. Instead, to apprentice oneself to Jesus, to follow him, means you are "with him, by choice and by grace, learning from him how to live in the kingdom of God. . . . Another important way of putting this is to say that I am learning from Jesus to live *my* life as he would live my life if he were me. I am not necessarily learning to do everything he did, but I am learning how to do everything I do in the manner that he did all that he did."[8]

THE ASPECTS OF THE HUMAN PERSON

"A person who is *prepared* and *capable* of responding to the situations of life in ways that are 'good and right,'" Dallas Willard tells us, "is a person whose soul is in order, under the direction of a well-kept heart, in turn under the direction of God."[9] A soul that is in order will integrate each of the aspects of the human person with all the others. These six aspects include the following:

1. *Thought* "brings things before our minds in various ways (including perception and imagination) and enables us to consider them in various respects and trace out their interrelationships with one another."[10]

2. *Feeling* "inclines us toward or away from things that come before our minds in thought. It involves a tone that is pleasant or painful, along with an attraction or repulsion with respect to the existence or possession of what is thought of."[11]

3. *Will*, or spirit or heart, is at play in what is chosen. It is the "capacity of the person to *originate* things and events that would not otherwise be or occur . . . *power to do what is good*—or evil."[12] We will not properly understand our politics, not to mention our lives, if we do not understand this aspect of what makes a human person a person. Without it, the idea of spiritual formation becomes nonsense. You have a spirit—an unbodily personal

power—right at the center of who you are and who you will become. This is your will. "The human will is primarily what must be given a godly nature and then must proceed to expand its godly governance over the entire personality."[13]

There is much to understand and explore regarding the interplay of thought, feeling, and will, and a full exploration is beyond the scope of this book. It is essential to make clear now, though, that your thoughts and feelings are not totally unchosen or completely removed from the influence of the will. In political behavior, and in much else, feelings are invoked as conversation enders—"Well, that's just how I feel"—or as justification for expressions of hatred and even violence. Sincerely and insincerely, feelings are used to rationalize antisocial political behavior. "We speak of feelings as 'passions,'" wrote Willard, "and that is a word that implies passivity. But we are in fact very active in inviting, allowing, and handling our 'passions.'"[14]

4. *Body* is the "focal point of our presence in the physical and social world. . . . It is our primary energy source or 'strength'— our personalized 'power pack.' . . . And it is the point through which we are stimulated by the world beyond ourselves and where we find and are found by others."[15]

5. *Social context* is the fifth aspect of what humans must and can do. Who we are is fundamentally related to our relationships—with God, but also with other human beings. The separation of our *social context* from spiritual formation has been truly harmful and has undermined spiritual formation itself. The affirmation of the social as a critical aspect of the human person, and therefore of spiritual formation, is at the heart of this book. "The power of our personal relations to others is what gives them their incalculable importance for the formation of our spirit and our entire life—for good, or for ill."[16] This is why we must tend

to the social, including the political. Any conception of spiritual formation that is limited to the private and internal is not credible.

6. *Soul* is "that dimension of the person that interrelates all of the other dimensions so that they form one life. . . . Because the soul encompasses and 'organizes' the whole person, it is frequently taken to *be* the person. We naturally treat persons as 'souls.' But of course the soul is not the person. It is, rather, the deepest part of the self in terms of overall operations."[17]

It is the interplay of these six dimensions that constitute the human self—who we are—and it is out of this interplay that our actions flow. "Spiritual transformation only happens," wrote Willard, "as each essential dimension of the human being is transformed to Christlikeness under the direction of a regenerate will interacting with constant overtures of grace from God. Such transformation is not the result of mere human effort and cannot be accomplished by putting pressure on the will (heart, spirit) alone."[18]

TRANSFORMING THE SPIRIT

So much of the Christian rhetoric and appeals to Christians in our politics today essentially amount to attempts at behavior modification. The instrumentalization of the Christian faith is a pervasive problem in our politics. People draw from the Christian faith to signal values or achieve an outcome, but often with the intent to leave its actual substance behind (we discussed this tendency on both the right and the left in chapter 3). It's a ubiquitous technique, and much of the time, it's not malicious and might even be helpful on some level. People in civic life may find some aspects of Christianity helpful, even if they have no interest in the faith itself.

It is genuinely useful that the Christian faith motivates volunteers to serve. It's useful that Christianity can promote family stability or ethical business practices or advocacy on certain issues. Concepts with a Christian history and charge, like hope and faith, have real rhetorical power and observable utility in our politics. In some sense, we should be grateful for this. Many civic leaders, many voters, in fact, may not believe or even have a construct for thinking that each human being is made in the image of God and is worthy of dignity and protection, but that doesn't mean we would be better off if they rejected the idea of human rights because they do not consciously buy into one of the most historically prominent and influential rationales for grounding those rights.

Still, we must not confuse the aesthetics of Christianity with the power to transform hearts and lives through interactive participation in the life of God. We also must reckon with the incoherency of wanting the things of God but not God himself. This is a problem with deep roots. We desire a politics of magic.

In his book *The Life We're Looking For: Reclaiming Relationship in a Technological World*, Andy Crouch describes the "fairy tale" of magic, though "unlike the fairy tales we tell to children, this is one that some of the smartest people in the world have believed in, dreamed of and tried to build."[19]

Obviously, Crouch's book focuses on technology, but the concept is both related to and useful in our context. "The quality that delights and intoxicates us in our technological devices," writes Crouch, "is the way they promise to work without us, without asking very much of us—like magic."[20] What magic allows for is the transformation of reality through means that are unrelated to their object. It is "impersonal power." "Magic" he goes on to say, "is about standing over, not under."[21]

"What technology wants is really what Mammon [the system that powers and is powered by technological magic] wants: a world of context-free, responsibility-free, dependence-free power measured out in fungible, storable units of value. And ultimately what Mammon wants is to turn a world made for and stewarded by persons into a world made of and reduced to things."[22]

Keep this in mind.

TWO CONTRASTING PORTRAITS

In Acts 8, we're told that Philip was preaching the gospel in Samaria. He performed great signs, Scripture tells us—driving out impure spirits in the name of Jesus, healing the paralyzed and lame. But Philip came to a people who were already enamored with a man who performed signs of a different kind and from a different source.

Scripture continues:

> But there was a man named Simon, who had previously practiced magic in the city and amazed the people of Samaria, saying that he himself was somebody great. They all paid attention to him, from the least to the greatest, saying, "This man is the power of God that is called Great." And they paid attention to him because for a long time he had amazed them with his magic. But when they believed Philip as he preached good news about the kingdom of God and the name of Jesus Christ, they were baptized, both men and women. Even Simon himself believed, and after being baptized he continued with

Philip. And seeing signs and great miracles performed, he was amazed.

Now when the apostles at Jerusalem heard that Samaria had received the word of God, they sent to them Peter and John, who came down and prayed for them that they might receive the Holy Spirit, for he had not yet fallen on any of them, but they had only been baptized in the name of the Lord Jesus. Then they laid their hands on them and they received the Holy Spirit. Now when Simon saw that the Spirit was given through the laying on of the apostles' hands, he offered them money, saying, "Give me this power also, so that anyone on whom I lay my hands may receive the Holy Spirit." But Peter said to him, "May your silver perish with you, because you thought you could obtain the gift of God with money! You have neither part nor lot in this matter, for your heart is not right before God. Repent, therefore, of this wickedness of yours, and pray to the Lord that, if possible, the intent of your heart may be forgiven you. For I see that you are in the gall of bitterness and in the bond of iniquity." And Simon answered, "Pray for me to the Lord, that nothing of what you have said may come upon me." (Acts 8:9–24 ESV)

Simon wanted the power of the kingdom of God without becoming the kind of person who would be fit for the kingdom. Simon was willing to use the language of faith, but not because he had a vision for a life of faith. Instead, he saw what Philip could do and wanted to do the same. Naturally—that is, out of his very nature—he sought to acquire this ability through transaction, not through personal transformation. Simon actually was not interested at all in the substance of the deed, but rather in the utility of the deed. He thought that with money, he could bypass actually becoming the kind of person who could do the things he saw the apostles do.

Peter identified this and told Simon to repent not for what he did but for "this wickedness of yours." Peter tells Simon to "pray to the Lord that, if possible, the *intent of your heart* may be forgiven you." Simon is so inattentive to his own heart, so unable to hear Peter's rebuke, that his plea in response makes little sense. He prays that nothing that Peter said would come upon him, but Peter's rebuke was about the very nature of his heart. Simon remained under the delusion that what did or did not come upon him, what he could or could not do, was a subject that was removed from the kind of person he was.

Immediately following the story of Simon in the narrative of Scripture, Philip comes across an Ethiopian eunuch—a man of significant status in charge of the treasury of the queen—who is seeking knowledge of the things of God as well. However, the eunuch's story is quite different from that of Simon's. Scripture tells us that the Spirit told Philip to go to the eunuch's chariot and "stay near it."

> Then Philip ran up to the chariot and heard the man reading Isaiah the prophet. "Do you understand what you are reading?" Philip asked.
>
> "How can I," he said, "unless someone explains it to me?" So he invited Philip to come up and sit with him. (Acts 8:30–31)

The eunuch proceeded to ask Philip, "Who is the prophet talking about, himself or someone else?" (Acts 8:34). Then Philip began with that very passage of Scripture and told him the good news about Jesus.

Scripture continues:

> As they traveled along the road, they came to some water
> and the eunuch said, "Look, here is water. What can stand
> in the way of my being baptized?" And he gave orders to stop
> the chariot. Then both Philip and the eunuch went down
> into the water and Philip baptized him. When they came up
> out of the water, the Spirit of the Lord suddenly took Philip
> away, and the eunuch did not see him again, but went on his
> way rejoicing. (Acts 8:36–39)

The eunuch learned the substance of what he desired first
and pursued it through means intrinsic to the desire itself. The
eunuch caught a *vision* of the gospel, clearly set an intention to
give his life to it, and took up immediately the *means* to do so.
And he was filled with joy!

POLITICS AS MAGIC

Our society, politics, and churches are hampered by a technological conceit—that we can attain the kind of society we seek
without coming to terms with the kind of people we are and
without becoming a different kind of people. Societal change—
real, lasting societal change—is not possible without coming to
terms with the nature of the problem. Our society produces mass
shootings at an unparalleled rate and scale, for instance, not in
spite of the kind of people we are, but because of the kind of
people we are.

Here is one place where the gospels of sin management
let us down and leave us wanting. These gospels have few

resources for critiquing Simon because Simon was more than open to affiliation and instrumentalization. He was more than willing to align himself with followers of Jesus and to "support the program." If they wanted him to raise his hand at the end of a sermon or sign up to petition a governmental policy, I'm sure he would have been happy to do so if he thought it would get him closer to what he wanted. Simon expected the apostles would be more than willing to accept him into the fold, regardless of the orientation of his heart, because Simon had influence and money. The value proposition was clear: Accept and affirm Simon, and he could help them achieve their goals. Did it matter if their motivations aligned? Philip would not be persuaded by Simon's offer of utility, however, and called Simon to repentance not for *improper action* but for the *intent of his heart.*

Our political life is full of acclaimed magicians who sell the promise of healing and improvement but whose heart's intent is self-aggrandizement. Wrongly, it is the eunuch we dismiss. How could we trust someone to lead who would take the counsel of a man running alongside his carriage? What kind of contribution could be made by someone who so readily admits his own ignorance? The eunuch has too little pretension, too little performance, for our politics today.

RENOVATION OF THE HEART

In *Renovation of the Heart*, Dallas Willard discusses what he calls "the general pattern of personal transformation."[23] This pattern is not specific to Christian spiritual formation. It is the pattern of vision, intention, and means (VIM). "If we are to be spiritually formed in Christ," Willard wrote, "we must have and implement the appropriate vision, intention, and means."[24]

It is a vision of our God-breathed world that can ground us. We can be captured by the real opportunity Jesus offers to live in his Father's kingdom with our friend Jesus. There is much talk of "co-laboring" with God, and increasingly we hear of "building for the kingdom," and these are generally good and biblical ideas. Yet recall my friend (mentioned in chapter 3) who expressed such personal concern about *the gap between what followers of Jesus profess and how we live*. That gap is the result of a message that includes profession, proclamation, and demonstration but leaves out formation. Willard wrote the following:

> Here, in a nutshell, is the explanation of the widespread failure to attain Christian maturity among both leaders and followers. . . . Those who are Christians by profession—and seriously so, we must add—today do not usually have, are not led into, the VIM that would enable them to routinely progress to the point where what Jesus himself did and taught would be the natural outflow of who they really are 'on the inside.' Rather, what they are inwardly is *left substantially as it was*, as it is in non-Christians, and they are left constantly to battle with it. That is why today you find many professing Christians circling back to non-Christian sources to resolve the problems of their inner life.[25]

Place this vision of life with Jesus before your mind and consider it:

Since, then, you have been raised with Christ, set your hearts on things above, where Christ is, seated at the right hand of

God. Set your minds on things above, not on earthly things. For you died, and your life is now hidden with Christ in God. When Christ, who is your life, appears, then you also will appear with him in glory.

Put to death, therefore, whatever belongs to your earthly nature: sexual immorality, impurity, lust, evil desires and greed, which is idolatry. Because of these, the wrath of God is coming. You used to walk in these ways, in the life you once lived. But now you must also rid yourselves of all such things as these: anger, rage, malice, slander, and filthy language from your lips. Do not lie to each other, since you have taken off your old self with its practices and have put on the new self, which is being renewed in knowledge in the image of its Creator. Here there is no Gentile or Jew, circumcised or uncircumcised, barbarian, Scythian, slave or free, but Christ is all, and is in all.

Therefore, as God's chosen people, holy and dearly loved, clothe yourselves with compassion, kindness, humility, gentleness and patience. Bear with each other and forgive one another if any of you has a grievance against someone. Forgive as the Lord forgave you. And over all these virtues put on love, which binds them all together in perfect unity.

Let the peace of Christ rule in your hearts, since as members of one body you were called to peace. And be thankful. Let the message of Christ dwell among you richly as you teach and admonish one another with all wisdom through psalms, hymns, and songs from the Spirit, singing to God with gratitude in your hearts. And whatever you do, whether in word or deed, do it all in the name of the Lord Jesus, giving thanks to God the Father through him. (Colossians 3:1–17)

POLITICAL VISION

What is your vision for our politics and your life in it? Do you have one? If so, what does it have to do with your vision of life in God's kingdom?

We've now arrived at a critical point where we must face and reject twin dangers. The first is that we must be clear in our minds that politics and our political life are not a worthy guide for our formation. Again, *it is Jesus who is the worthy focus of our spiritual formation, the trustworthy shepherd of our souls, the safe resting place for our hearts.* There can be no confusion on this point. It is not that we must become the kind of people our politics needs because our politics needs it. It is that our politics desperately needs people who have put away anger, rage, malice, slander, and filthy language (Ephesians 4:31). Our politics desperately needs people clothed with compassion, kindness, humility, gentleness, and patience (Colossians 3:12). We are not pursuing formation for the sake of our politics; rather, our pursuit of formation in the likeness of Christ naturally addresses the ills and needs so widely recognized in our public life.

The second danger is that we completely miss the fact that life with Jesus is for all of life, including politics, and we make political decisions as if they are outside of the realm of God's concern or resources. This danger is a form of political idolatry too. We make an idol of politics when we set it above God *and* when we set it apart from God.

Instead, avoiding these twin dangers, imagine how your formation in Christ might be lived out in the circumstances and areas in which your life touches politics. What do you imagine would be characteristic of our political life if God's will were to increasingly have its way on earth in our politics and public life as God's will is perfectly realized in the heavens? What might people do in our politics, and what might be done through our politics, if this were to be so? What is your vision for our political life and your interaction with it?

We should not be captured by this, or any, political vision; we should be captured by the vision of our God-breathed world, which is overflowing with God's care for us, for you. This vision gives us eyes to see all else. It allows us to see that we can carry a kingdom heart with us into all of life, including politics. This results not in a discrete policy platform but in an overall character, a kind of disposition, that affects everything else.

"Seeing God for who he is enables us to see ourselves for who we are," Willard wrote. "This makes us *bold*, for we see clearly what great good and evil are at issue, and we see that it is not up to us to accomplish it, but up to God who is more than able. We are delivered from pretending, being presumptuous about ourselves, and from pushing as if the outcome depended on us. We persist without frustration, and we practice calm and joyful noncompliance with evil of any kind."[26]

Now that is a godly vision we can take into politics! Imagine how our politics would change if we had citizens who decided that they would approach politics as a part of their overall commitment to "persist without frustration" in practicing a "calm and joyful noncompliance with evil."

What is your vision for our politics and the kind of person you would like to be in it? I encourage you to pray about this and to keep this question in mind as you go about your life. Consider the vision I have offered here, as well as the various visions offered by Christians over the years, such as the notion of a Beloved Community, the model of good governance offered in the murals of the Palazzo Pubblico in Siena, and many, many others.

As should be clear by now, the more prescriptive the vision becomes regarding actual arrangements, the more loosely it should be held. However, these visions can inform and inspire your own vision. Godly vision gives birth to moral imagination. We must not be aimless in our politics. We must have some vision in our sights. What is yours?

OVERTHROWING POLITICAL SECTARIANISM

There is certainly more to a holistic vision of a godly politics than rejecting and upending the political sectarianism we discussed in the opening chapter of this book, but there is certainly not less than that. Rejecting political sectarianism will not necessarily lead us to hold the most desirable policy positions, but we underestimate the extent to which political sectarianism practically consigns us to holding less desirable policy positions and having a dysfunctional political process. Political sectarianism offers us nothing of value, and it robs us of so much. We can do without it.

You will remember the three pillars of political sectarianism: aversion, othering, and (misplaced) moralization. The person of Jesus, and the life he offers to us, has every resource for overthrowing the structures of political sectarianism. His way of life does this, not as an instrumental reaction to the harms of political sectarianism, but simply by its nature. The goodness of Jesus' vision for the way we treat one another, for the kind of people we can become, simply overwhelms the impulses of political sectarianism.

Aversion

Whereas aversion teaches us to dislike and distrust those who disagree with us politically, Jesus was radically open to those who were not considered by others to be "on his team" for one reason or another. Consider his own disciples, who were drawn from the other side of lines of division in the society of his day. Consider the Samaritan woman at the well (John 4), the woman with the alabaster jar (Matthew 26), or the centurion whose faith was unlike any Jesus had found in Jerusalem (Matthew 8). Jesus' teachings were consistent with the life he lived.

> You have heard that it was said, "Love your neighbor and hate your enemy." But I tell you, love your enemies and pray for those who persecute you, that you may be children of your Father in heaven. He causes his sun to rise on the evil and the good, and sends rain on the righteous and the unrighteous. If you love those who love you, what reward will you get? Are not even the tax collectors doing that? And if you greet only your own people, what are you doing more than others? Do not even pagans do that? Be perfect, therefore, as your heavenly Father is perfect. (Matthew 5:43–48)

We are tempted by many voices in our politics to believe that it's foolish, impossible even, to seek the good for those who do not seek the good for us. This is, of course, the story of human history. It is a story Jesus interrupted for our sake, and his way offers an exit ramp off the highway of retaliation, revenge, and resentment. His life provides us with the imagination we need to reject aversion.

Othering

Othering is a terrible rejection of the dignity of the human person. It is a degradation not only of its object but also of its purveyor. It is a denial not only of the person's innate dignity but also of God, for all human beings have been made in God's image. In Jesus' world, the distinctions that so typically prompt othering are overcome.

Scripture directly ties formation to this new social reality: "But now you must also rid yourselves of all such things as these: anger, rage, malice, slander, and filthy language from your lips. Do not lie to each other, since you have taken off your old self with its practices and have put on the new self, which is being renewed in knowledge in the image of its Creator. Here there is no Gentile or Jew, circumcised or uncircumcised, barbarian, Scythian, slave or free, but Christ is all, and is in all" (Colossians 3:8–11).

James Catford, one of Dallas Willard's friends and the founding chair of the Center for Christianity and Public Life, says that "wherever we draw the lines in society—about who is acceptable and who is unacceptable—Jesus is to be found on the other side of the lines."[27] May God help us stand alongside Jesus.

Moralization

The trouble with moralization in politics is that it too easily leads to the ultimatizing of penultimate issues. Combine the moralistic tendency with othering and aversion, as political sectarianism does, and you have a system in which great harm can be justified and perpetrated. Disagreement, or even a difference in emphasis, can prompt condemnation because of the moral weight given to one's own political opinions.

Now, of course, there are political opinions that must be strongly rejected, and we should not coddle truly abhorrent political views or even political actors with significant influence who wield that influence to advance malevolent causes in our politics. *The absence of moralization does not require the absence of conviction.* Moralization is about what you do with your opinions. Do you consider your political opinions to be sacrosanct? Do you view political disagreement as license to condemn?

We are not careful enough with condemnation. The demands for condemnation of and among those of public notoriety have now trickled down into regular human affairs. It's not only the national decision-maker who must be condemned for their political actions or opinions, but your uncle or grandmother as well, who may not even bother to vote but who nonetheless simply does not have the correct political views. For some, if a person's political opinions, or even the absence of an opinion, can be tied to a harm or injustice, nearly anything can be said about their motives or character.

"When we condemn another," Willard writes, "we really communicate that he or she is, in some deep and just possibly irredeemable way, bad—bad as a whole, and to be rejected. In our eyes the condemned is among the discards of human life. He or she is not acceptable. We *sentence* that person to exclusion."[28]

This will sound familiar to anyone paying attention to our political discourse, the press releases that flow from attention-seeking advocacy groups, and the political figures desperate to get on cable news. What's worse, if you aren't willing to go along, to affirm and reissue the condemnation, you become suspect.

Willard describes how to correct without condemning. He isn't talking about politics here, of course, but his guidance is worth considering in the context of politics, even if it is not perfectly applicable and will require adjustments when considered in this area of life.

First, "we don't undertake to correct unless we are absolutely sure of the sin."[29] Immediately, this presents real challenges when applied to politics since it can be so difficult to assess the motivations, circumstances, reasoning, and effects of a politician's actions. When it comes to the average citizen, to our neighbors, the complex nature of politics can complicate the process of correction in a different way. With a politician you might reserve judgment (and correction) because it is possible they know something you do not, while with your neighbor it might be apparent that they do not understand the implications of their political action.

Second, "not just anyone is to correct others. Correction is reserved for those who live and work in a divine power not their own. For that power is also wise, and it is loving beyond anything we will ever be."[30] How often do we see condemnation used in our politics and in social life today by those who are haunted by the idea that they themselves might be subjected to condemnation for their own political failures and poor judgment? Perhaps if others are marked as more deserving of condemnation, it will never arrive at their doorstep ("At least I'm not *that* bad!").

Our impulse should be the opposite of this. Perhaps someone *is* worthy of correction, but am I the one to make it? What would be my purpose? Not just some grand ideological purpose, but what is my real purpose *for this person* with my correction? We would cut much of our condemnation off before we could issue it if we stopped to consider this question first. Remember the words of Jesus: "Do not judge, or you too will be judged. For in the same way you judge others, you will be judged, and with the measure you use, it will be measured to you" (Matthew 7:1–2).

Third, "the 'correcting' to be done is not a matter of 'straightening them out.' It is not a matter of hammering on their wrongness and on what is going to happen to them if they do not change their ways. It is a matter of *restoration*."[31] Herein lies the fundamental distinction between correcting and condemning. Condemnation is never about restoration. Correction can be open to restoration, but the condemnation of a person is, by its nature, closing the door to restoration. Right correction comes from an earnest desire for its object to "get back on track."

Fourth, and finally, "the ones who are restoring others must go about their work with the sure knowledge that they could very well do the same thing that the person 'caught' has done, or even worse. This totally removes any sense of self-righteousness or superiority, which, if it is present, will certainly make restoration impossible."[32] In the realm of politics, it is helpful to think of political history and the fact that nearly any historical figure of note held at least one view that would be condemned today. Indeed, think of your own history and some of the views you used to hold and regret today.

This model of correcting rather than condemning is helpful in thinking about both our activity and our expectations regarding politicians, especially when it comes to our social interactions. It may be appropriate to argue that a politician should never serve in public office again. This is a kind of condemnation—of the "politician" at least, if not necessarily of the "person." Still, it may feel like a total condemnation to the person. We should be careful that we don't allow our hearts to revel in someone's personal destruction, even if it is the result of a definite political action that is fair and justified.

This idea of moralization brings to mind the apostle Paul's discussion in Romans 14. Here, Paul discusses other prudential matters. Dallas Willard's discussion of judgment seems to draw directly from this passage:

One person considers one day more sacred than another; another considers every day alike. Each of them should be fully convinced in their own mind. Whoever regards one day as special does so to the Lord. Whoever eats meat does so to the Lord, for they give thanks to God; and whoever abstains does so to the Lord and gives thanks to God. For none of us lives for ourselves alone, and none of us dies for ourselves alone. If we live, we live for the Lord; and if we die, we die for the Lord. So, whether we live or die, we belong to the Lord. For this very reason, Christ died and returned to life so that he might be the Lord of both the dead and the living.

You, then, why do you judge your brother or sister? Or why do you treat them with contempt? For we will all stand before God's judgment seat. (Romans 14:5–10)

Be wary of a hubris in political life that might put you in the judgment seat that is God's.

INTENTION

We now have the imagination for a politics that rejects the impulses of political sectarianism. However, we should not confuse ourselves by thinking that because we have a vision for our politics—or for our own lives, for that matter—we *stand for* that vision. The gap between our vision and our intention is manifested in phrases such as, "Wouldn't it be nice if . . ." or "In an ideal world . . ." We can have a vision in mind without actually planning to conform ourselves to it.

Once we have in mind a vision for the kind of politics we could have and the kind of person who could contribute to it, we must actually intend to be(come) that kind of person. A decision must be made.

In intending to become the kind of person whose life would line up with a vision, it can be helpful, necessary even, to consider what kinds of feelings and behaviors would flow from a person who was living in light of such a vision in particular circumstances. Do any of these feelings or behaviors seem undesirable or impractical to you? If so, it may be a sign that your vision needs refinement. Or it can help you identify where your heart and mind do not truly "believe" your vision, and you can decide whether you *want* to believe your vision and to become the kind of person called for by that vision. It will do you no good to have a vision for politics and your place in it if you don't want to work toward that vision. You may decide, however, that your vision is worth pursuing and that while you may not currently "want" to be the kind of person it would require, you want to change your "wanter."

Jesus is prepared to help us see our good intentions through challenging circumstances. When we make the decision to be the kind of people who, for instance, reject political sectarianism and a politics of antagonism, we look to Jesus and ask for the Holy Spirit's guidance in fortifying our intention for moments when we would otherwise question the possibility of such a commitment. Jesus' yoke is easy because he is strong. He has seen faithfulness through to the end.

"When Jesus deals with moral evil and goodness, he does not begin by theorizing," Willard explains.

> He plunges immediately (Matt. 5:21–44) into the guts of human existence: raging anger, contempt, hatred, obsessive lust, divorce, verbal manipulation, revenge, slapping, suing,

cursing, coercing, and begging. It is the stuff of soap operas and the daily news—and real life.

He takes this concrete approach because his aim is to enable people to be good, not just talk about it. He actually knows how to enable people to be good, and he brings his knowledge to bear upon life as it really is, not some intellectualized and sanctified version thereof.

He knows that people deeply hunger to be good but cannot find their way. No one wishes to do evil for its own sake, we just find it unfortunately "necessary." We want to be good but are ready to do evil, and we come prepared with lengthy justifications.[33]

Politics is not the only area of life in which we, unfortunately, find doing evil necessary, but it is an area of life in which the necessity of doing evil is too easily and openly affirmed. The logic of this easy affirmation creeps into the private and personal parts of our lives. But Jesus stands with us against it. He is faithful to help us see our holy intentions through as we are captured by a vision of his kind of life. And he honors even our fumbling efforts to follow him.

Chapter 7

SPIRITUAL DISCIPLINES FOR PUBLIC LIFE

The eternal life, from which many profound and glorious effects flow, is *interactive relationship with God and with his special Son, Jesus, within the abiding ambience of the Holy Spirit*," Dallas Willard wrote in *The Great Omission*. It is "the Kingdom Walk, where, in seamless unity, we 'Do justice, love kindness, and walk carefully with our God.'"[1] You learn this walk through apprenticeship to Jesus—by *learning from Jesus how to live your life as he would lead your life if he were you*. We are captured by this vision, and we intend to pursue it.

Recalling the previous chapter, let us proceed as though you and I have reached the conclusion that we do not want our political activity to be guided by the logic of political sectarianism, that such a politics does not flow from a Christian life. Further, you and I are taken up by a vision of politics as loving service, and we have decided that insofar as our lives touch on politics, we will become the kind of people who would act in accord with a spirit of loving service. We seek to be formed in this way in relation to our politics because we are convinced that it is consistent with following Jesus with our whole life. What might we do now?

Take note that the decision we have made is not simply an intellectual or emotional conclusion that a politics of loving service is preferable in some abstract way to political sectarianism. The decision is not one of preference or wishing or acknowledgment that "it would be nice if . . ." The decision is one of purpose. We intend to become that kind of person. That intention is formed in prayer and discernment—an intention made in concert with our expectation and prayer that God will bless it and help us as we follow through on it.

The intention alone is insufficient because while we are now the kind of person who would *intend* it, we are not yet the kind of people who would or could *do* it, certainly not in the most demanding circumstances or environments. Indeed, political sectarianism itself—the logic of aversion, othering, and moralization in our politics—is itself a demanding environment. Dallas Willard wrote, "If I intend to obey Jesus Christ, I must intend and decide to become the kind of person who *would* obey. That is, I must find the means of changing my inner being until it is substantially like his, pervasively characterized by his thoughts, feelings, habits, and relationship to the Father. The means to that end are not all *directly* under my control, for some are the actions of God toward me and in me. But some are directly under my control."[2]

Let us now turn to those means.

SPIRITUAL DISCIPLINES

A discipline is an "activity within our power that we engage in to enable us to do what we cannot do by direct effort."[3] Spiritual disciplines help us be "active and effective in the spiritual realm of our heart, now spiritually alive by grace, in relation to God and his kingdom. They are designed to help us withdraw from total dependence on the merely human or natural (and in that precise sense to mortify the 'flesh,' kill it off, let it die) and to depend also on the ultimate reality, which is God and his kingdom."[4]

In *The Spirit of the Disciplines*, Dallas Willard provides two basic categories of spiritual disciplines: those of abstinence and those of engagement. Disciplines of abstinence involve the planned, temporary forgoing of the satisfaction of normal, even healthy, desires. Abstinence involves purposeful self-denial so that we might "bring these basic desires into their proper coordination and subordination within the economy of life in [God's] Kingdom."[5]

Disciplines of engagement involve the taking up of certain activities. If disciplines of abstinence generally "counteract tendencies to sins of commission . . . the disciplines of engagement counteract tendencies to sins of omission."[6] Both kinds of disciplines are required, and they work together as "a proper abstinence actually breaks the hold of improper engagements so that the soul can be properly engaged in and by God."[7]

In and through it all, Jesus is at the center. We follow Jesus' lead into any practice we take up, and we seek to learn from him in the midst of these practices. We know that we are not saved by these practices, just as we are not saved by merely holding the right ideas about God or the right views regarding issues of social justice.

Relatedly, the point of spiritual disciplines—and the aim of spiritual formation—is not behavior modification. Our principal aim is not what we do but *who we become*. We "aim at the heart and its transformation. We want to 'make the tree good.' We do not aim *just* to control behavior, but to change the inner castle of the soul, that God may be worshiped 'in spirit and in truth' and right behavior cease to be a *performance*."⁸ *Create in me a clean heart.* This is the cry and desire of the psalmist, the longing of the disciple.

One of the reasons Jesus' yoke is easy and his burden light is that he is helping us become the kind of people who can do what we want to do. Imagine! What a profound, extraordinary difference this would make for so much of life today. Remember the extraordinary discovery we made earlier regarding life in the kingdom: *Jesus offers the only kind of life that is free from the need to perform.* Our hearts and our actions can be ever more aligned in goodness. This is the grace of God made available to us.

In the remaining pages of this chapter, we'll discuss various disciplines that counter some of the negative impulses in our political life. Remember, though, that we're not after a check-list of behaviors, but rather a kind of life. A life that develops in such a way that we will be able to respond in politics ever more appropriately, as though Jesus were standing right there between us and the person we are talking to, standing right by our side as we consider the issues confronting our communities.

SPIRITUAL DISCIPLINES TO OVERTHROW POLITICAL SECTARIANISM

We know that our political environment today inspires aversion, othering, and a misplaced moralization, and so we begin there, with disciplines that will indirectly form in us the kind of hearts that will resist those impulses. We will find that the Christian faith has tremendous resources that can resist, and ultimately overthrow, political sectarianism.

Fellowship over Aversion

As a reminder, aversion is the tendency to dislike and distrust those who disagree with us politically, particularly those in a different political party. This aversion is toxic for our politics, but as we've seen, it creeps into the communion of believers as well. The very thing that ought to make Christians identifiable to the world—our love for one another (John 13:35)—is overridden by our politics, thus undermining the testimony of our faith.

Of course, if in the midst of a politics of aversion we find the possibility of fellowship among believers of various political backgrounds realized, it likewise would be both a gift to our politics and a shining testament to the love of God realized in and among his people.

Throughout my life, I've seen aversion at play and have been subjected to it as well. I don't know which is worse—to be subjected to this aversion as a young, impressionable new believer or as a believer of twenty years with a testimony of God's work in my life. I've dealt with both.

What makes it all the more difficult is that the feelings are intense, but the knowledge that undergirds those feelings is profoundly limited. The aversion of our political sectarianism is not rational, and so when it is supported as a matter of religious adherence, both the faith and the politics become a house of cards. That's what it was like for many young Christians who grew up in Christian households that hated the Clintons, that treated the Clintons as paragons of vice, only to become apologists for Donald Trump. I hear from young Christians regularly about how disorienting this was, not principally to their politics, but to their faith. It was aversion in action.

The problem is not reasoned opposition. Aversion does not refer to reasoned, strong opposition. Aversion describes the immediate, intense dislike and distrust of someone because of their political affiliation, regardless of other factors, including a shared faith.

How wonderful it has been, then, to be a part of many relationships and environments in which Christians are choosing fellowship over aversion. Perhaps most significant in my life over the last several years is to see the incredible examples and testimonies that have emerged from the community of young political professionals organized by The Center for Christianity and Public Life since 2021. This community includes members spanning political, denominational, and cultural differences, as well as those who work for members of Congress in different parties and for advocacy organizations with competing agendas.

We pray together, read Scripture together, encourage one another, hear from one another (as well as from elder believers), study and worship together, and celebrate together. We learn from one another, though the community is not a forum for advocacy or debate on political issues. Instead, there is an awareness of the uncertainty that runs through so much of our work—the knowledge of our own imperfections—and that, too, creates a different kind of solidarity within the group. Through fellowship, not only have members of the group stayed *in* community with one another, but they also have increasingly become *for* one another. Fellowship centered on Jesus has made aversion less plausible and God's reality more tangible.

Our experience offers not only an example for fellow citizens of how to transcend the politics of aversion, but I anticipate that tremendous civic contributions will flow from communities like this as people in positions of influence refuse to be the kind of people who simply go along with the logic of aversion. They are a different kind of people.

Service over Othering

Othering can be deterred by fellowship, but there is a distance implied by othering that is not present with aversion, which leads me to propose *service* as the appropriate counteracting discipline. Fellowship is simply not possible, at least not immediately, with some—including, of course, non-Christians but also people with whom we may have a history or a preexisting boundary that makes fellowship unrealistic in the short term.

In service, "we engage our goods and strength in the active promotion of the good of others and the causes of God in our world."[9] Service is not always a discipline. We may serve simply as a natural outflow of a spirit of love and righteousness. However, one might also "serve another to train myself away from arrogance, possessiveness, envy, resentment, or covetousness."[10] I am adding to that list the terrible, dignity-denying tendency to "other" and "view opposing partisans as essentially different or alien to oneself."[11]

Service, particularly service in environments or for recipients that run counter to one's politics, can undermine the othering tendency. I know a pastor who was raised in a politically conservative family. Without really deciding to, he came to hold the background assumption that real Christians are either politically conservative or deluded. This view held up not only when dealing with social issues like abortion, but also when it came to a basic acceptance of conservative, partisan attitudes regarding economic policies, including the belief that government aid to the poor typically harmed rather than helped the poor.

Then he was given an opportunity to plant a church in an economically impoverished city. After he spent some time pastoring in the community, welfare recipients were no longer abstractions to him, but rather his congregants and his friends. He counseled people who were seeking to gain greater economic security but had to rely on government support to make it to tomorrow and the next day. Glib political narratives about "government moochers" and "welfare queens" were not only more difficult to accept wholesale intellectually; they were personal and had to do with people he knew personally. Not only did he serve them, but—and this is the thing about service—he had been served by them.

The point here is not that this pastor arrived at the right political views. I don't know for sure if his actual policy views changed one iota, though new experiences in new environments often do lead to changes in a person's politics. Regardless, his politics was no longer undergirded by distant judgment and dismissal of the needs, interests, and dignity of others through "othering"; instead his heart toward people and a whole range of political interests and issues changed.

I also know progressives who entered into service with the belief that their perspective was completely aligned with those they would serve. They read all the "right" books and voted the "right" way, after all! How unsettling it was to find that the sympathetic abstractions they had in mind were confounded by actual people. They went to serve in communities wrecked by violence, expecting to have their calls for defunding the police met with resounding "amens," only to find that many of those who were closest to and most affected by violence wanted an increased police presence, even as they were certainly not sanguine about police. They met local activists who believed that school choice was a social justice issue. Through service, they came to understand that justice as conceived by those they were serving, the people they believed they were representing, didn't always fall neatly along the red-blue divide.

Instead of following the lead of a few loud voices, they had to learn to actually listen to diverse voices, people who didn't have a policy vision perhaps, but who did have a point of view based on their life experience. Through service, they came to understand that our politics is not always as simple as "siding with the poor" because "the poor" are not a political monolith. Instead, they would have to take responsibility for their own positions and be open to refining their views even further, based on new information and new experiences.

Some progressives I know who have had experiences like this changed their views on some issues. Others did not change the positions they hold but did change the way they hold them, and they aren't so quick to advocate for their views in ways that dismiss the differing perspectives they came across in their service experiences.

Engaging in service is perhaps most important for those in leadership positions or positions of privilege. However, service can be a vital discipline for those who feel like they have nothing to offer or, more specifically, like they have nothing that those they disagree with politically would possibly want. This is especially true in the context of othering. It turns out that those the world counts as undesirable, those who never receive recognition, often have much to offer in service. Through service, status is disrupted, and the categories of those who contribute and those who receive can be turned upside down enough that we can see one another more clearly. With the new sight of service, the perceived offensiveness of the other can be transformed into the offensiveness of othering at all.

Confession over Moralization

Moralization is "the tendency to view opposing partisans as iniquitous," or particularly sinful.[12] As with the other pillars of

political sectarianism, many spiritual disciplines can help cultivate resistance to a misplaced moralization in politics. Service
and fellowship certainly can play a role. Confession, too, can
be crucial by keeping in front of us the reality of our sinfulness
before God. As we confess our sin to God and to one another, we
not only remember our sinfulness but we are also reminded of
the tenderness with which we hope to be received.

It is yet one more sign of the dehumanizing nature of our politics that it could lead us to so callously, so wantonly, cast people
aside. It is one thing for non-Christians to appeal to politics as
the decisive indicator of one's righteousness. For Christians to
use mere party affiliation as the ultimate criteria of a person's
goodness is, by design or gullibility, to supplant the purposes of
God with the purposes of political power. Confession can teach
us to take sin seriously enough that we wield accusations of sin
with humility and care when it comes to the complicated, contingent realm of politics.

This challenge of moralization in our politics is cause to
recall a conversation we had in chapter 4 regarding our views
of God. I sense that much of the moralization in our politics
flows from a view of a punitive God who is stuck with human
beings he created but doesn't like very much—those with whom
he is tremendously disappointed. This kind of view is held by
many Christians, as well as by those who claim no religious
affiliation but nevertheless are influenced by who they imagine
God to be.

To them, God is a gray cloud looming over them with judgment, holding them to a standard they could never reach and
mercilessly grading their failure. The fixer gospel comes to these
people as a kind of loophole in the system of a merciless God.
Whether they accept that gospel or not, God remains a dour

figure who is eager to condemn. Politics provides an arena where we can be in the seat of the judge, making determinations about the iniquity of our political opponents. And some people wish to be as harsh with their political opponents as they feel God is harsh with them—a vision of God that must be corrected in their minds. As Dallas Willard put it, "The fondness, the endearment, the unstintingly affectionate regard of God toward all his creatures is the natural outflow of what he is to the core—which we vainly try to capture with our tired but indispensable old word *love*."[13]

To the political moralist who is so used to condemning on the basis of "political iniquity," the discipline of confession might be viewed as punishment. If you approach confession with the anticipation not of merciless punishment but of grace-filled embrace, confession will transform how you view yourself and those around you. You may even find that you become less prone to quick condemnation based on political disagreement.

OTHER SPIRITUAL DISCIPLINES FOR OUR POLITICAL LIFE

There are other classic, time-tested spiritual disciplines through which God can meet us and help us become the kind of people our politics needs. I will briefly discuss some of the disciplines and how they might relate to our political life, but remember that this is not a universal, one-size-fits-all program. What I hope is that this discussion will lead you to think about your own life, how you relate to politics, and what disciplines God might be calling you to take up. Crucially, attend to your heart as you do this.

Solitude and Silence

Solitude and silence are essential disciplines that push back against some of the most destructive attitudes and impulses in our politics. In solitude, "we purposefully abstain from interaction with other human beings, denying ourselves companionship and all that comes from our conscious interaction with others."[14]

"Solitude frees us," Dallas Willard wrote.[15] Solitude frees us from the need for others' approval to justify our existence. Solitude frees us from the noise of our politics and the monied forces vying for our attention and adherence. In solitude, we can be reminded that we exist apart from the constant sustenance of others' opinions and the endless stream of inputs and distractions that make up so much of our lives. It can be quite shocking to find that just a day in solitude can open up space in our thoughts and feelings and provide new perspective. Away from the clutter and bluster vying for our attention, we discover that we have a soul. We discover a God who cares for our soul, and we can retrain our heart to focus on him.

In solitude, we refrain from interaction with other human beings, while in silence, we intentionally seek the absence of manufactured noise, including our own talking. Silence can be terrifying. We are comforted by noise. Different noises make us feel fun, productive, in control, alive. What do we hear in the silence? Who are we there?

Solitude and silence are disciplines that can break the chains of performance. They provide separation from the never-ending assessments of others and the unthinking adjustments we make in response to social cues and requirements. They help us reset our social and political tendencies.

Remember our discussion of Dietrich Bonhoeffer's idea that we never meet another person one-on-one? Silence and solitude can renew this vision in our minds. We will reassess our behavior and outlook in the social realms and can identify where we didn't see God and where we didn't invite him. We may realize how often the impulses of aversion, othering, and moralization—not to mention anger, resentment, pride, and fear—are incited by our political and social environment rather than inherent and unavoidable responses to reality.

Secrecy (or "Anonymous Service")

With the discipline of secrecy, we "abstain from causing our good deeds and qualities to be known."[16] As Dallas Willard himself acknowledges, the term *secrecy* isn't quite right—we are not referring to secrecy of any kind or for any purpose, but instead a specific kind of secrecy. I prefer the term *anonymity* or *anonymous service* to describe this discipline.

Regardless of the term we use, this discipline is vital for our political life, since it can help us "lose or tame the hunger for fame, justification, or just the mere attention of others. . . . We learn to love to be unknown and even to accept misunderstanding without the loss of our peace, joy, or purpose."[17]

Our political life turns every good deed, every quality, into something to be traded and considered a kind of capital. Favors are given with the expectation that they will be reciprocated. Positions are taken with the expectation they will stymie criticism. This applies to those not in political jobs as well, of course. We announce our donations to a political cause in order to ingratiate ourselves with a certain group of people. We put the banner up on our social media pages. We make a show of our rejection of certain ideas or people.

Again, these things are not necessarily bad or evil. Politicians rightly need to be aware of the ways in which they let people know about good things they are doing, since they are accountable to the people in their work. More donations are inspired when you share that you donated to a cause, and communicating where you stand on an issue can help influence others in a positive way. However, what I've found is that it's far too easy for the attention we receive to make us lose sight of our actual convictions, motivations, and purpose. Would you support a particular cause or take a particular stance if it did not affect your social standing or career prospects? How does acting in politics (donating, volunteering) anonymously, thereby avoiding recognition, change the way you feel about your political action? Talk with God about it.

Secrecy as a discipline is especially helpful in politics because of what we discussed in chapter 4—the problem of credit in politics. If you have practiced the discipline of secrecy, you may find yourself more willing and able to both identify and take up political action that is oriented toward the good, even if it is unclear how identifiably decisive your action will be in the fate of a particular process. Why? Because you're acting in service of a cause that is greater than yourself, and that's worth it, whether people know you're doing it or not.

Two final notes before we move on. First, this discipline does not supply permission to be a social media troll through an anonymous account. The discipline of secrecy is about resisting the temptation to make our good deeds known, not about being belligerent under the cover of anonymity. Second, and relatedly, this spiritual discipline involves secrecy absent deceit. We do not mislead people. The core of anonymous service is about the orientation of our hearts. The discipline is to purposely avoid recognition in a particular instance or for a particular period. If the mere idea makes you feel anxious or conflicted, do not take up this discipline until you've settled those issues in your heart through prayer and possibly consultation with a pastor, friend, or trusted advisor.

Study

Dallas Willard describes study as the "chief positive counterpart of solitude."[18] Where "solitude is the primary discipline of abstinence for the early part of our spiritual life, so study is the primary discipline of engagement."[19] As we study Scripture, first and foremost, and also "the lives of disciples from all ages and cultures of the church," we feed our faith, grounded in knowledge, and become ever more aware of and awakened to the work of God in our own lives, in the lives of others, in the church, in history, and in nature.[20] We study, not to acquire trivia or to immerse ourselves in meaningful sentimentalities, but in the pursuit of knowledge about reality. Study is for and about life.

We can and must draw on this knowledge for public life. The spiritual discipline of study is a tremendous resource for resisting the empty promises and false premises we are so often tempted by in our politics. Without study, we will bring to the public a fragile insecurity in what we are supposed to believe as opposed to a joyful confidence about what we know. Study is essential to humility, perhaps counterintuitively, for a person who is dispositioned toward learning is inherently aware that they have more to learn.

Worship

Study "opens the way for the disciplines of worship and celebration," according to Dallas Willard. "In worship we engage ourselves with, dwell upon, and express the greatness, beauty, and goodness of God through thought and the use of words, rituals, and symbols."[21] In worship, we give careful attention to and are taken up with the worthiness of God, and as we worship, God takes up greater space in our lives.

Through worship, we recognize God for who he is and therefore put all else in its proper relationship to him, including our politics. Through worship, we affirm the ultimacy of God and therefore the penultimacy of politics. In communal worship among politically and culturally diverse people, we can gain an imagination for what it would be like to order our affections in light of the greatness of our God. Right worship is a bulwark against political idolatry.

Celebration

"We engage in celebration," Dallas Willard writes, "when we enjoy ourselves, our life, our world, *in conjunction with* our faith and confidence in God's greatness, beauty, and goodness. We concentrate on *our* life and world as God's work and God's gift to us."[22]

Celebration as a spiritual discipline is the great testament to Christian hope. Like worship, it quiets idols and rightly situates our lives and our circumstances—including our politics—in relation to God and his kingdom.

There is concern in some quarters today that celebration undermines social change, and that to celebrate is to affirm the status quo. Celebration, though, is an affirmation of life in God's kingdom, and it is both sustenance to those who partake in it and a testament to a reality with profound implications for how we order our lives politically. Celebration, particularly the celebration of those who are enduring injustice of some kind, marks an unwillingness to deny the goodness of God and our worth in God's kingdom in the face of powers and systems that run counter to it. "Holy delight and joy is the great antidote to despair and is a wellspring of genuine gratitude,"[23] and it is from that wellspring that injustice is made out to be the great sham that it is.

PRACTICES FOR OUR POLITICS

In addition to time-tested spiritual disciplines, through prayerful consideration, we can engage in practices and modes of engagement or abstinence that are particular to politics.

News Consumption

Christians are often concerned about how to approach the news in a healthy and constructive way. I receive questions about this topic at nearly every speaking event. It comes from two directions—from those who are newly interested in politics and want to know where to start, and from those who feel the way they have been consuming news media has not been healthy for them and they want to change.

Here is some general advice. First, *read broadly*. People often ask me for the best source to get "neutral, unbiased" news. While I believe the idea of objectivity should not be discarded by journalists, I do believe we should stop looking for that holy grail of news that is "just the facts." One reason is that we are not very good at discerning which news outlet is truly shooting straight, but our desire for that has become the subject of news brands and advertising campaigns that appeal to that desire. Instead of looking for the one trustworthy outlet, I recommend reading a limited but relatively broad set of news sources and publications spanning the political spectrum. By doing so, you'll learn not only how differing political perspectives look at the same issue but also how people of differing political perspectives often pay attention to entirely different issues and events.

Second, *read deeply, not anxiously.* You can't read everything, and you certainly can't follow every story. While you may feel compelled to reflect on why you're not interested in certain topics or stories—and you may find you need to change—I tend to think that so long as your reading is not totally dictated by self-interest or a shallow search for entertainment, it's best to allow your instincts and interests to have a say. If you find an issue or aspect of government that you feel particularly called to care about, follow it closely. Read deeply about it, keeping in mind the advice above to read broadly about that same issue.

Know also which news stories simply aren't worth your time, at least not yet. It is not unusual that the story taking up the headlines of the day is more gossip than actual news. I tend to wait until allegations are substantiated or investigations come to an official close before dedicating too much attention to them. I also try to remind myself that the more extraordinary a political charge is and the more seemingly straightforwardly a political actor casts their opponents' motivations or intentions, the more hesitant I should be in running with that narrative.

Reading the news shouldn't be just one more thing you're supposed to do but don't do and then feel guilty about it. You may have seasons in your life when spending twenty minutes reading the news doesn't just feel like a chore; it feels impossible. That's okay! Perhaps those seasons are opportunities to express openness to different perspectives in conversation with others, acknowledging that you might not be attuned to the finer points of a particular debate.

Third, *read locally.* Your political influence and responsibility are typically most significant in your local area. A number of challenges face local news operations today, but to the best of your ability, strive to support and pay attention to local news about the political decisions and needs of your local community.

Fourth, and finally, *read the news as an invitation to prayer*. In 2022, I started a simple podcast series called *The Morning Five*. The show features roughly five-minute episodes every Monday through Thursday that open with Scripture and conclude with prayer, with a brief summary of the day's headlines in between. My goal is to build up Christians' expectation that God is not distant from the news we hear and read every day. God is not distant from history. God moves in history. And in all of this we can take our concerns and hopes about our political life to him.

Prayer

I want to offer a word about prayer here, since we're on the subject, though it certainly could have been covered earlier in this chapter. Prayer is an essential spiritual discipline for our political life. It is unfortunate that prayer has become a subject of political debate, hashtags (#thoughtsandprayers), and dismissive asides from news anchors and politicians in reaction to the perceived misuse of prayer to deflect responsibility or play a kind of identity politics (a perception that is sometimes justified).

It's particularly unfortunate that some Christians have naively treated criticisms of prayer as benign while totally embracing a critique of prayer in the context of politics and current events. I understand that prayer is sometimes invoked by politicians in the absence of certain forms of political action on some issues. Those who appeal to prayer disingenuously to serve their own interests will receive what is due to them.

Some invocations of prayer might be so obviously and transparently self-aggrandizing that they can be critiqued on a case-by-case basis. Christians, though, should be sure that in their frustrations over the misuse of prayer, they do not lend credence to the idea that prayer is useless or that it somehow prevents the "real" action from taking place. We must not be so reactive that in our opposition to the misuse of our faith we become unwitting partners in efforts to mock or otherwise undermine the concepts and practices that are core to the faith itself.

Dallas Willard rejects this thinking outright: "How misguided are those who regard prayer as irrelevant to social conditions! No doubt many things called 'prayer' are quite useless in every respect, but nothing is more relevant to social conditions than the transformation of persons that comes from prayer at its best in the life of the disciple of Christ."[24]

Prayer has sustained and informed some of the greatest social movements in human history. In the Christian life, prayer and action are complementary, not at odds. However, make me choose, and I'll take any day the faithful prayers of a Christian whose heart desires justice over the keyboard warrior cursing at politicians' accounts on Twitter and calling it activism.

Breaking Groupthink

If we're honest, political conversations in our families or among friends, when not defined by conflict and animosity among their participants, often serve the purpose of making the opinions of others less intelligible and more unthinkable. It can feel good to have our political views affirmed by those we respect and love. We can ingratiate ourselves and build intimacy with others while creating distance between our group and those on the "outside" by constantly affirming the rightness of our group. The hearth of our shared political views creates great warmth among us, while the distance of others puts them farther and farther out into the cold. The outworking of these dynamics can quickly become primal, vicious, and costly.

Now, I wouldn't advise anyone to become a stick in the mud or an aimless devil's advocate. However, you might as a practice of formation make it a point to raise what you honestly consider to be legitimate, troubling critiques of the position around which your group consolidates itself. Rather than the repeated ritual recitation of shared grievances and shared solutions, you can interject the interests or perspectives of others. Indeed, by doing so, you will bring to the surface the hidden doubts you yourself hold on the issue—hidden from the group for fear of rejection or perhaps even hidden from yourself. Introducing other perspectives might be difficult at first. You may have to work at even becoming familiar with the kinds of objections to your position that others hold—a task that may require other kinds of disciplines or practices. But doing so can be an edifying process in and of itself.

The discipline of breaking groupthink can play out in a number of ways. The objection you raise may be one that can be easily overcome, and in that case, at least you and your conversation partners will have punctured the insulation of your echo chamber with the consideration of others. Ideally, though, you will come upon an objection to your group's point of view that is not easily discarded. Whether or not the objection should prompt a change in position depends, obviously, on the specific case. Regardless, what can be cultivated is a sense of *humility* regarding the political judgment your group has made and *respect* for those with whom you disagree. Your conversation may naturally bend toward addressing the objection. The political actions that flow from such a conversation would be more other-centered than they otherwise would have been.

Surely, depending on the group, you may risk rejection for even raising a contrary perspective, and interrupting the pleasure of groupthink. But you know that pleasure sours, and its fruit turns bitter over time.

Bearing One Another's Burdens

In the afterword to my first book, *Reclaiming Hope*, I discuss the apostle Paul's encouragement to "bear one another's burdens" (Galatians 6:2 ESV), and I suggest the spirit of this calling can be wisely applied to our politics and public life.[25] One way to do this is to apply the same basic kind of practice described in the last section to our interactions with public officials and other political leaders—that is, to use the resources, skills, status, and access you have to give voice to and advance the interests of those whose interests are either different from or even opposed to your own.

This practice isn't reserved for the elite and powerful. You can implement it right now. Write a letter to your city councilperson or member of Congress about an issue or point of view you believe needs greater consideration—one that is not a matter of personal gain. You might even write about a concern that is primarily held by those who oppose your ultimate position on an issue, but that you would like the public official to consider as they act.

For instance, you may think, at the end of the day, that a school voucher program is a wise policy. However, you hear concerns from people in a different social position than yours that such a program would harm public schools. You don't have school-age children, and you believe the benefits of the voucher program outweigh these potential harms, but you're not certain. Your state representative supports the voucher program, and so you're in agreement on that, but you take seriously the concerns you've heard about the potential harms of such a program. You could write your state representative and note that you are their constituent and that you ultimately support a school voucher program. That said, as their constituent and as a voter, rather than dismissing criticisms of the voucher plan, you want the legislature to substantively address concerns about the program because they are now your concerns too. You expect the state representative to do what they can to determine the validity of those concerns and to take appropriate action to respond to valid concerns.

You can imagine this same kind of action in different settings and on different issues. Perhaps instead of writing a letter, you would be able to address your question to a public official directly. Or you might decide to donate to a worthwhile event of an organization you generally disagree with politically. The point, beyond the immediate, practical effect of the action you're taking, is that you are training yourself to view politics through the lens of not just your own interests, but the interests of others. You are training yourself to operate in politics in response to something more, something greater, than self-interest or the narrow interest of your party or ideological circle.

Civic leaders, even at the top levels of our politics, can do this as well, though it requires courage and a commitment to public service rather than devotion to self-aggrandizement. One example that comes to mind is that of Senator (and onetime US presidential candidate) John McCain. At a major campaign rally just weeks before Election Day, McCain fielded a comment from a supporter who said, "We're scared of an Obama presidency." McCain replied, "First of all, I want to be president of the United States, and obviously I do not want Senator Obama to be. But I have to tell you, he is a decent person, and a person that you

don't have to be scared [of] as president of the United States."
McCain was booed for that comment—at his own rally, no less.[26]
Obviously, it suggests something about the emotional and psychological state of our politics that people would boo the idea that they do not have to be scared. And this was in 2008!

Affirm Those You Oppose; Critique Those You Support

Finally, as you look at your social media feeds or other avenues through which you share your political views, assess the tone and content of what you have shared. What is the overall mood of that content? What does it reflect about you? Generally speaking, if your last ten political posts are about how great your side is and how awful your opponents are, it's a pretty good sign that you are captive to, and contributing to, our culture of political sectarianism. What might it look like to disrupt that habit?

You can take up the practice of sharing articles that make strong arguments against the position you hold. You can actively acknowledge when a politician from the other party does something you support. You can actively state your disapproval of something your side does. What if one out of every ten political posts you sent broke from the partisan mold? Doing this wouldn't be a performance on your part, but rather a reflection of your thinking and the views you hold. The performance, the fantasy, is that one party, one ideology, has 100 percent of the answers 100 percent of the time. Leave the persistent partisanship to those who actually work for political parties. That's their job. Unless you work for a party or a candidate, it's not yours.

We could discuss any number of other disciplines and practices, of course. In fact, the list is endless. We are experimenting in partnership with our Good Shepherd, Jesus, who leads us through our distractions and our foibles and our disobedience.

In *The Spirit of the Disciplines*, Dallas Willard suggests that those who are used to the "better things in life" can "do grocery shopping, banking, and other business in the poorer areas of the city. This has an immense effect on our understanding of and behavior toward our neighbors—both rich and poor—and upon our understanding of what it is to love and care for our fellow human beings."[27] Think about how our politics might change if this practice were taken up by a significant percentage of the population.

As this chapter draws to a close, I want to give three warnings to help prevent you from draining the life out of discipleship:

First, *you must avoid a burdensome legalism with all of this.* Remember, this life of following Jesus is full of grace—not just for your failures but for your successes as well. All of it is grace. This is not a new project you must rush through; it's not an exam on which you are graded. God is not disappointed in you. He is not befuddled by how "behind" you are. He delights in you. Discipleship is not a cost Jesus demands in exchange for heaven; discipleship is the best life on offer.

When it comes to spiritual disciplines and practices, you do not need to punish yourself with endless journaling if journaling does nothing for you. Don't approach spiritual formation as an endless drudgery that God requires for his pleasure and your misery. You are working with God, and he with you. If you want to learn to pray so that prayer is edifying for you, ask God to help you with prayer. Talk with him about things you can try together, and try those things—and then talk with him about how it went.[28] I promise you that God wants you to have a joyful and confident prayer life.

Second, *all of these teachings are meant, first and foremost, to be applied by you to yourself.* I believe that politics is causing spiritual harm in the lives of Americans largely because Americans are going to politics to get their spiritual and emotional needs met. I hope you, reader, will think about ways that might be true in your life. What I don't intend, what I don't think would be helpful, is that we would routinely apply these standards or modes of analysis to other individuals in the heat of political life.

We should not be quick to accuse a person who passionately makes their case on a political issue that they engage in politics to get spiritual and emotional needs met. I do believe that party identity can become an idol, but we should be hesitant to use the accusation of idolatry as a way to rebut a person's argument. We must be humble about our own perceptions, and especially careful when it comes to these matters of character, motivation, and the state of individuals' souls as we interact with them in our politics and public life. *We can do great harm if this language of spiritual formation becomes just another tool for political warfare.*

The nature of the public square makes it nearly impossible for personal assessments of this kind to be made in and perceived as good faith. Even in private interpersonal exchanges, it is typically best to talk with the person as they present themselves and their ideas, at least for a while, before addressing the connection between their political ideas and the kind of person they are.

Finally, *a spirit of competition will crush whatever good can be done through the VIM (vision, intention, means) pattern of personal transformation*. Part of what we are learning from Jesus is to not think of ourselves as better than our fellow citizens— Christian or not. While we are confident in the resources available to us as Christians, we welcome the civic contributions of others. We all know people who do not share our faith who are not only exemplary citizens but are also capable of greater displays of generosity, gentleness, or kindness in our public life than we are. Our involvement in public life is not a competition, and we are not anxious about proving ourselves. We are certainly not anxious about proving anything about God.

We are not seeking to acquire a status or privilege in our civic life as we live out our commitment to take seriously the ways in which the kind of people we are affects our politics. We approach politics, and people in politics, in the spirit of loving service. Always.

A WEEK IN LAURA'S LIFE

To conclude this chapter, let me show you what it looks like to take up spiritual disciplines for public life. I'll use a fictional example of a particular person with a particular life during a particular season. Again, our purpose is not to take on the burden of a list of activities to add to our checklist to try to earn God's favor or to burnish our reputation. We are asking Jesus how we can be faithful in the entirety of our lives, and we are experimenting with the means to follow through on our intention to be the kind of person who can be faithful in political and public life.

This is Laura's intention. Laura is a thirtysomething married mother of two children with a full-time job outside the home. She has always been interested in civics, but in recent years she has become increasingly concerned about the nature of our politics and how it is affecting her family and her community. In the past, Laura didn't necessarily intend to separate her Christian faith from her politics, but she was wary of all the ways in which connecting faith and politics could go wrong, and so she never really committed to be a Christian in her political life. Of course, some of the positions she took were influenced by her faith and she generally thought of herself as a decent person, but she had never really connected the dots.

Now, though, she felt like the time for connection had come. She wanted to pursue the good of her neighbors through political involvement. So for months now, she has intentionally sought guidance from the Lord as she has taken up practices to learn how to follow Jesus in her political life. Here is what that looked like for Laura this particular week.

On Sunday, Laura had signed up to lead in prayer that morning. Many people at her church knew she may not have voted for her state's governor, and so it surprised some that she would pray for the governor and the administration, that they might serve the state and its people well and be protected and blessed by God. Laura also prayed for the nation of Myanmar, which was in the throes of a political crisis with significant human rights implications. Several members of the congregation who hadn't heard about the crisis in Myanmar—and hadn't specifically thought about whether God cared about what was happening in Myanmar—were prompted by Laura's prayer to donate to a Christian nonprofit serving in the country.

Following church, Laura, her husband, and their children volunteered at a local food bank after reading a news article about a specific community in their city that qualified as a food desert—an area where local schools were reporting that students had inadequate access to food. While volunteering, Laura spoke with workers at the food bank and folks from the neighborhood and learned more about the challenges the community was facing. Some of the people said that crime was a significant issue in their city and that it might even be connected to the hunger issues they were facing.

That evening, Laura's husband took care of the kids while Laura took her monthly evening of solitude and silence to seek the Lord in advance of a busy week.

On Monday, Laura shared an article she had read on Sunday night about crime prevention on her social media account. She wasn't totally convinced about the article's conclusion, and she made that clear, but she also said some of the arguments in the article were worth considering.

Tuesday was Election Day. Laura was able to take a half day off from work and volunteered to drive voters to the polls. She volunteered through a local church, and she was sure that not all of the people she picked up were going to vote the way she voted. *What better way,* she thought, *to support the principles of democracy and to recognize the dignity of the people I'm serving than to aid in their civic participation, regardless of how they will vote.*

Laura had spent time researching the candidates as best she could in the midst of her busy life, and she prayed that she would use her vote in a way that would best steward the limited influence she had for the good of her neighbors. There was no way to express with one vote all of the valid concerns and opinions she heard at the food bank earlier that week, but she considered them as she made her decisions in the voting booth.

On Wednesday, Laura read the local newspaper and learned that the mayoral candidate she supported won. The mayor-elect announced he would prioritize addressing homelessness, and so

Laura sent an anonymous donation to a homelessness nonprofit that would likely serve as a vital partner for the mayor's effort. Laura also wrote the mayor, noting that she had been a supporter and sharing the news article on crime she had read on Sunday. She admitted that crime hadn't been one of her top political concerns, and she wasn't sure she agreed with everything in the article, but she told the mayor the issue had come up too often in her conversations for her to ignore it any longer. She expressed her hope that the mayor would visit the food bank to talk with folks there as she had, and that he would take concerns about crime seriously and consider solutions and policies offered by people who hadn't supported his election as she had.

On Thursday, Laura and her husband were studying Scripture together. They had been interested in learning more about the fruit of the Spirit, and it hit them that they had never considered the role that patience can play in political life. They concluded they had more or less dismissed patience in politics as a euphemism for complacency, for not properly valuing, to quote Martin Luther King Jr., "the fierce urgency of now." However, now they wondered if perhaps patience in politics looked like steadfastness, a refusal to close the door on a possibility prematurely. They decided to raise the issue with friends and explore it further.

On Friday, Laura fasted. She came up with an idea months ago to ask her church to host an evening event on hunger issues in their city, but she didn't have the capacity to organize it herself, so she worked with church leaders to commission a fellow church member, a younger woman she had been mentoring, to lead the organization of the event. Laura chose to fast that day as she prayed that the Lord would use the event for his glory and for the good of the community.

The event that evening was amazing. The young woman who organized the event decided, in part based on the article Laura had shared on Monday, to invite an expert on criminal justice issues to serve on the event panel, along with experts on the issue of hunger. The church had invited the mayor-elect to attend the event, but he could not make it. Laura was therefore surprised when one of his top aides approached her at the event to let her know that the mayor had read her letter and had asked the aide to attend the church's event to see what they could learn. The event was attended by both church members and interested community members. The pastor overheard comments from one attendee that they didn't know Christians cared about the community beyond "getting people saved."

On Saturday, Laura and her family hosted a cookout with friends. They celebrated a busy week. They thanked God for all he was doing in their lives and in their community. They caught up with one another and played a big, unruly game of football together. In the evening, they sat around a fire and took up the question Laura and her husband had been discussing about patience and what it meant to become patient people in all the various roles they had—spouses and parents, bosses and employees, congregants and neighbors—and, yes, as citizens.

Chapter 8

TO PARENTS AND PASTORS

In this chapter, I'll address two groups that have been under strain as a result of the interplay of faith and politics—parents and pastors. Parents and pastors carry special responsibilities when it comes to both spiritual formation and the flourishing of societies. While so many feel burdened, both parents and pastors need to reclaim the dignity of their callings. Both parents and pastors need to be encouraged.

SPOKESPEOPLE FOR CHRIST

Dallas Willard concluded *Knowing Christ Today* with a chapter addressed specifically to pastors and what he referred to as "teachers of the nation" and "spokespeople for Christ."[1] He was primarily referring to pastors, but he was also addressing leaders of Christian organizations and, really, any Christian in public who is readily identified and associated with Jesus.

As teachers of the nation, pastors are "the ones who, by

profession at least, have the knowledge that must be taught to meet desperate human need."[2] Their task is "*not* to get people to believe things, to share 'Christian' feelings or rituals, to join Christian groups, or to be faithful to familiar Christian traditions. . . . The task of Christian pastors and leaders is to present Christ's answers to the basic questions of life and to bring those answers forward *as* knowledge—primarily to those who are seeking and are open to following him, but also to all who may happen to hear, in the public arenas of a world in desperate need of knowledge of what is real and what is good."[3]

As we discussed in chapter 2, it has been debated whether Christians have knowledge that is even relevant to the public and to the functioning of the "real world." While you'll find many Christians who bemoan the "changing culture," their noises too often amount to nostalgic protestations, a pining for a past in which they believe Christian knowledge was assumed and welcomed. The past they long for was likely not as welcoming or Christian as they seem to imagine, and the present they bemoan is not as closed off to Christian knowledge as they seem so ready to concede. The questions are all live and up for grabs. The time to contend for the credibility of Christian resources in public life is now, and the task must be taken up by spokespeople for Christ now for the good of the public.

For pastors and others to do this, they will need to have knowledge of truth and reality. "It is not enough," wrote Dallas Willard, "that pastors identify what the right doctrines are and that they believe them or are committed to them. They must know them to be true and must be living according to the realities they represent."[4] This is not a call to muster up certainty; quite to the contrary, it is a call to be honest. It is knowledge of reality based in lived experience as an apprentice to Jesus yourself that will allow you to be joyfully confident in what can be a disorienting world.

From this place, pastors must present the knowledge they have as "knowledge that can be verified by individuals who have an interest and will invest the time and effort required to do so."[5] Pastors must choose to occupy this role with intelligence, gentleness, and humility, to be sure, but they—you!—must choose it. It is a calling of great dignity and purpose to which you have been called by God.

The alternative, and what is understood by many Christians and non-Christians as the current role of the pastor, is to teach what Christians are supposed to believe (perhaps what they had better believe). Among Christians who hold this view, then, the pastor's success is judged by professed conversions and raised hands. To the outside world, and among Christians as well, success is achieved through a pastor's tactics and charisma. Pastors are called on to establish a culture, to make a value proposition, to inspire, but never, in some contexts, to offer knowledge about reality. In lieu of an expectation of knowledge, pastors are expected to provide entertainment and keep folks "engaged." Their calling to make disciples has turned to a mandate to create consumers. It's exhausting. So many pastors simply become exhausted.

There is another way—"Paul's way"—in which, wrote Willard, "presenting knowledge as knowledge, spokespeople for Christ do not try to manipulate the hearers' feelings or actions in any way. They can lay down the burden of getting people to do things. They know that passion comes from reality and simply do their best to help willing hearers understand and come to know the reality and goodness of life in the kingdom of God with Jesus."[6] They make disciples of Jesus, people who are learning from Jesus how to live their lives in light of the eternal life Jesus offers.

The local congregation is central to the making of disciples. "The most important thing that is happening in your community," said Willard, "is what is happening there under the administration of true pastors for Christ."[7] Life with Jesus entails life in community with other Christians, for "only the personal and corporate dynamics of such a group are suited to be the place where humans learn to [in Jesus' words] 'love one another as I have loved you.'"[8]

This is the crux of it. It's a high calling. It is Jesus' plan. And it brings us to politics. Not politics alone. Not politics primarily. But to politics nonetheless.

"Real life, 'ordinary' life," Willard wrote, "is the place of disciples and the place of discipleship. There disciples 'reign' in the office, laboratory, farm, the schoolroom as well as in media, sports, the fine arts, and so forth. They reign for what is good in the home, the community, and in voluntary and involuntary associations of all kinds, even up to international organizations and relations. They effectively care for the goods of human life that come under their care and influence."[9]

One of the convictions that drove me to write this book is to argue, from the depths of my being, that we must reject the fatal choice between a Christian silence in politics and a Christian subservience to political programs, ideologies, and aspirations. Both of these paths make the Christian message incoherent. To follow either path will strip us of our integrity as spokespeople for Christ. These two approaches, which flow from the disappearance of moral knowledge, suggest to the public and to Christians that "there is no 'there' there" when it comes to Christianity; that real life is no place for discipleship.

PASTORS AND THE POLITICAL PROBLEM

Still, it's easy to understand why many pastors want to keep politics out of the life of the local church because when politics gets in, it's often destructive to community and a burden on pastors themselves. A 2022 Barna Research study found that 39 percent of Protestant clergy had considered quitting full-time ministry in the last year. Thirty-eight percent of those clergy who had considered quitting cited "current political divisions" as a factor. When the Barna Group followed up with those who had cited politics, a majority expressed concern that "Christians are more loyal to their political views than their faith."[10]

Politics has been enormously disruptive to the goals of growing and managing local churches, recruiting and retaining staff, building diverse and healthy Christian communities, maintaining and growing tithes and other revenue, and much more of what has come to be the work of a pastor. If churches are businesses with the goal of selling a product to potential consumers and they are judged by whether they get folks to buy the product without regard for what they do after the "purchase," I think I'd agree that trying to avoid politics is the best strategy. It would be risk mitigation in pursuit of a market objective.

Pastors are not, however, selling a product, but rather are offering knowledge for the purpose of making disciples. In a culture such as ours, in a polity in which birth grants citizenship, whole-life discipleship requires discipleship in the realm of politics.

Pastors are not obliged to issue pronouncements and orders regarding every political decision that has to be made. In fact, part of political discipleship is understanding the nature of what Christianity offers to our politics, and an irrefutable, singular "biblical" policy agenda is not included in that. Sometimes Christianity is relevant to our politics because we learn from it what politics is not and what politics cannot accomplish.

Dallas Willard wrote the following:

The unity of humankind through the unity of God imposes an inescapable demand. The unity of humanity is a genuine moral imperative upon modern humanity that expresses itself in many ways. It is a crying need to which secular humanity tries to find a remedy by social and governmental arrangements of ever increasing scope and intensity. But the unity required is beyond attainment by human beings on their own. It can be achieved only "under God," for it is a unity of love. Otherwise, the "moral" imperative of human unity becomes a blood-soaked curse upon the earth at the hands of those who would *force* their way upon others. And "ethnic" distinctions of one kind or another always come into play in coercion to regimented uniformity rather than genial coalescence into organic unity. What has happened in recent decades in Rwanda, Bosnia, and Sudan is not a fluke or some strange thing. It is a natural outcome of what is in the human heart. If you are going to "give peace a chance," you must radically change the human heart. It must be ruled by love under God, founded upon knowledge of God.[11]

Here Willard is not alleging that government and politics are without value or utility. He's also not saying that politics is irrelevant to the furtherance or hindrance of "human unity." But whereas so much of our culture sets politics as the farthest horizon, the primary instrument for social transformation,

Willard sets politics in perspective. In this case, in this context, he does it this way. In cases in which people seek to claim not *too much* responsibility for politics but *too little*, a different emphasis will be needed. To model the relevance of Christianity to our political life is not the same thing as using Christian language and ideas to coerce a particular political action or adherence to a specific policy agenda.

This is often what is demanded or expected of pastors. I hear from pastors regularly whose inboxes are full of people asking them to speak out on this or that issue or implying that the pastor had a partisan motive where there was none. Sometimes these "requests" come with threats that if the pastor does not speak or otherwise act as the church member demands, they'll leave the church or stop giving money.

It is a rare occasion when a congregant will make political demands without the expectation of a specific political outcome. If you are a pastor and you receive an email from a person who wants you to speak out on a particular political issue, it is possible the person is genuinely interested in what you have to say and eager to embrace whatever you have to offer on the subject. It is much more likely that the person making the request isn't seeking knowledge, but rather advocacy and authority. They want the weight of pastoral authority, and the biblical authority implied with that, to settle the argument they've been having with someone in their small group. They want to be able to say, "You heard the pastor. I'm the one with the Christian view on that." Be discerning and humble, pastor. Do not trade your authority as a minister of the gospel for the fleeting and fickle influence of a political pundit.

I do not believe there is a one-size-fits-all approach to speaking about politics from the pulpit. Some traditions and church cultures expect that the pastor will speak to ways to interpret Christian principles for application to particular political debates, and it is generally understood that the pastor does this in a different mode and with a lesser authority than when teaching biblical doctrine, for instance. Pastors should not assume that their congregants or the watching world know this, however.

If pastors shouldn't ignore politics and shouldn't pose as political pundits or strategists, what should they do?

Again, allowing for diversity of many kinds, here are some general recommendations.

First, *use the political and cultural conversations of the day as a prompt to connect the needs and desires that those conversations reveal to God's heart of love for all people.* Pay attention to what happens in the spirits and dispositions of your congregants as you raise issues that touch on politics or public life.

When you bring up politics in your preaching, it should not regularly serve as a way to reinforce a sense of community (which often actually excludes members of the church, unless all political diversity has already been purged). Do not ignore the kinds of emotions and reactions that you solicit when you discuss political or cultural issues. Remember, it is not enough—it is not even really the goal—to convince your people to have the right position, if they are unable to hold it in the right way. If there is something that must be affirmed, affirm it. If there is something that must be critiqued, critique it. But do it all with love, not as an aloof scoffer. Our politics is bearing tremendous human need right now that it cannot fully satisfy, but we do not gloat or take pride in the inadequacy of politics.

Instead, identify movements, actions, and people that in some way reflect God's heart. Tell stories of faithful Christians in the past who have engaged in politics for good, even if imperfectly. To identify the good in politics or a political act is not to endorse it as God's perfect will. The pastor does this not to lift up mankind, but rather to lift up God.

Teach that politics is an arena for faithfulness now as it has been in the past. Teach about Daniel and Esther, Augustine and Aquinas, William Wilberforce and Olaudah Equiano, Jacques Maritain and Fannie Lou Hamer. Be always on the lookout for ways to encourage hearers with glimpses of God at work through his people and in the midst of the morass and pain of public life. Perhaps there are people who work in politics or civic life in your own congregation. Pray for them and provide them with opportunities to serve as resources for the church. Have the courage to identify some aspect of God's heart in current political events, not to advance a partisan cause, but to enliven your people to a kingdom at work, to show them possibilities for good.

You may battle a tendency, a reflex, to analyze each reference in light of how it may work out in terms of partisan or ideological interests. While it is good to be aware of flash points and the immediate political environment, one aspect of what you're teaching Christians is to look for God first in politics rather than worrying that every utterance could shift some partisan balance of power.

Over time, with God's help, they will become the kind of people who are glad to hear good news and affirm the good before making any partisan analysis. They will be able to hear the story about John McCain referenced in the last chapter, for instance, and their internal monologue will not be about whether the story is intended to suggest he would have been a better president than Barack Obama or that Barack Obama was so wonderful that he elicited kind words even from his opponent—or any other number of motivations.

I will be able to write, as I did in my previous book, that I was grateful that then-Senator Ben Sasse, a Republican from Nebraska, would regularly say he believed politics was not ultimate, without Christian readers immediately speculating as to whether my citation meant I agreed with Sasse on this or that policy issue or wanted people to vote for him.[12]

Second, though, is that *I do not believe it is essential for pastors to regularly address political issues in their sermons, and the pressure and motivation to do so is significantly alleviated by addressing political issues and needs in other aspects of the service.* While I understand that various formats are used in church services, and I've attended and benefited from churches with different kinds of liturgies, I must say I have found little of greater value regarding this topic than time for communal prayer. In some traditions, the nation's president, no matter who they are, and local and state elected officials will be prayed for by name. The language of the prayer is consistent, regardless of the political party or current political standing of the politician. This exercise is deeply formative. Similarly, it is powerfully formational and instructive for Christians to be guided to pray in response to significant international, national, and local current events. Done well, such prayers can help cut off the vindictive, spiteful, and soulless impulses our political culture can prompt and reorient the ways in which Christians relate to specific developments. Over time, these prayers shape how Christians relate to politics in general.

Third, *think outside of Sunday mornings as you look for ways to encourage your church community to cultivate a healthy Christian approach to politics.* If you do not want to address politics from the pulpit on Sunday, it can be helpful—and alleviate pressure on Sunday morning as well—to provide other forums where your congregants can reflect on politics and public issues. Host small groups that cover these topics. Sponsor events featuring Christian speakers who will address political issues in a way that is edifying. Provide opportunities for members of your congregation to interact with politicians and elected officials by hosting forums. Partner with government and other institutions to find ways your church can serve your community.

Fourth, *model ways in which Christianity transcends and confounds political frameworks and show that Christians can be active participants in civic life, not just passive recipients of what politics offers.* We've touched on this a bit already, but I want to offer a few additional examples specifically on this point. We discussed Christ the King Sunday in chapter 4, and that day on the liturgical calendar conveys precisely this transcendent and confounding capacity of Christianity in the face of typical political expectations and paradigms.

I also like an idea developed by The AND Campaign, a Christian civic organization—led by my friend Justin Giboney—of a church questionnaire that includes questions about general issues of Christian political concern that do not uniformly favor one political party over another. The questionnaire can be used in many different ways, but I think church leaders can put it to greatest use by requiring any politician or candidate who asks to speak at their church to fill it out.

Now, it is certainly acceptable for churches to simply have a blanket policy against allowing politicians to speak or be introduced at their church, but for those that do typically allow it, an unfavorable dynamic could result. A politician might step up to the pulpit, quote Scripture that a staffer prepared for them, ask for prayer for the upcoming election, and leave achieving what they wanted to achieve without ever having addressed any critiques or issues of concern that church members may have. By requiring use of this questionnaire, a pastor or other church leadership would inform a politician that they'd be happy to host them so long as they provided answers to the questionnaire. The church could make the politicians' answers available to members. The pastor could even follow up on some of the answers. By proceeding in this manner, the church enables an exchange, an engagement, to take place and plays a proactive role in shaping the terms of that engagement. I advocate that every church that hosts elected officials and candidates during its gathering should use this questionnaire or one similar to it.

PARENTS

According to a 2022 *New York Times* survey, nearly one out of every five American adults reported that they recently had a political disagreement with a family member or friend that hurt their relationship.[13] I hear regularly from parents who are concerned about their child's politics, and whenever I speak at a college or high school, I know I will get at least one question about navigating political disagreement with parents.

The problem is easily overstated. According to American National Election Studies data from 2020, only 34 percent of Americans report that political differences had hurt family relationships in the previous four years, and only 16 percent said those differences caused a "great deal" (3 percent), a "lot" (3 percent), or a "moderate amount" (10 percent) of hurt.[14]

Even if most American families aren't being torn apart because of politics, a significant number of families are strained by politics, and every American family needs to navigate political conversations. As Christians, parents must be thinking about politics because politics is and will be a part of their children's lives and the way they live out their faith.

It's in the context of family life that we develop our intuitions regarding politics and its place. Is it off-limits and something that should not be discussed? Does politics come up as a source of grievances? Self-interest? Social concern?

How and in what ways are your political views conflated with your faith? Can you help your kids think Christianly about politics, even if it leads them to decisions that are different from yours? Or is that inconceivable to you?

I have a four-year-old daughter, and I'm amazed at her ability to catch my inconsistencies. She will remember if I said I was going to do something but don't do it. She'll recall a rule I instituted in one scenario for one purpose (often for my personal convenience) when I institute a different, contradictory rule in another circumstance (again, usually for my personal convenience). Does anything make a parent of a young child more proud and more ashamed than when your child asks you to behave in a way that is consistent with the way you expect them to behave?

Teens and college students notice and remember the inconsistencies in their parents' stated values and the interesting dynamics of what happens when politics enters the picture. I've met too many Christian college students over the years who have been thrown into doubts about the faith they were raised in because of a perceived lack of congruence between their parents' faith and their politics. It's rarely simply an issue of which people their parents voted for or which positions their parents held, but rather it's often more about how they held those positions and the things they said to explain their political stances.

Much of what will help the parent-child relationship when

it comes to politics is covered by discipleship, with the aid of the resources and ideas in this book. My primary guidance to parents is to accompany your child in their political searching and development with patient interest and Christian resources that can support their development. Establish an environment in which it is naturally assumed that Jesus has something to offer when it comes to the issues of our day. I suggest, similar to my advice for pastors, that you pray with your children about current events. Read stories to them about Christians who made a difference in political life. Point out when something that reflects the heart of God shows up in our political life.

A friend recently reached out to me for advice regarding his teenage son. His son was (somewhat unexpectedly) developing political interests, and though he didn't agree with his son's emerging ideology, his real concern was that his son's political interest seemed to have been prompted by a rather vitriolic and judgmental influencer. The influencer was entertaining and always had a clever put-down for those who disagreed with him. "It's not the healthiest or most balanced presentation" of politics, my friend told me.

My advice to my friend was that with gentle humility, he could recommend to his son various ways he could test out some of his emerging political ideas through civic involvement. What might it look like for his politics to help people in practice rather than just in theory? Actual political involvement opens up organic opportunities to contend with the various ways the influencer might be eliding a more complex reality with his entertaining but crass and disparaging approach. The heart of a political hobbyist is always directed inward. Civic action provides the opportunity for our political ideas to move out and be shaped by reality and by negotiation and partnership.

Above all, politics is a forum for discipleship, for cultivating in your children a joyful confidence in God.

Pastors and parents have high callings. They, you, will play a significant role in determining the course of history. You are just the kind of people God had in mind.

Of course, they aren't the only ones. We were *all* made to make a difference.

Chapter 9

THERE WILL BE A DIFFERENCE

I've tried to be especially careful not to speak excessively about what outcomes could be expected should we allow Christian resources to influence our politics and our own civic participation. We are not taking up Christian spiritual formation to achieve a political outcome. However, as we draw to a close, it is necessary to offer what I can regarding what is possible in light of all that we have discussed.

It is fair, I admit, to look out at a politics that is full of grand "promises" and easy "solutions" and ask, "What difference could I possibly make?" In a politics of monied interests, power players, complicated processes and procedures, technology and data-driven manipulation, and so many other structural impediments to real change, what good is spiritual formation?

RETURN TO ROBERT COLES

Robert Coles, you will remember from the second chapter, is the Harvard professor and child psychologist who was at a loss when confronted by a student who asked him, "I've been taking all these philosophy courses, and we talk about what's true, what's important, what's *good*. Well, how do you teach people to *be* good?"

In 1986, Coles wrote *The Moral Life of Children*.[1] In the book, he describes his theories about why children behave the way they do and talks about the id, the ego, and the superego and how they interact with one another. And yet his theories were confounded by one little girl named Ruby Bridges.

At age six, Ruby Bridges was the Black student who initiated school integration at the William Frantz School. The school was integrated as part of the response to the Supreme Court's decision in *Brown v. Board of Education*, which was decided in 1954 just months before Ruby's birth. By 1960, integration was required in Louisiana by a federal court order, but it continued to face intense resistance from both public officials and White citizens.

For months, Ruby was escorted by federal marshals as she made her way to her local public school. For nearly a full school year, she was the sole student at William Frantz, as White families boycotted, refusing to send their children to school with a Black student. Every day, marshals escorted Ruby through a mob of angry people who would curse her, shout racial slurs, and hurl death threats. On Ruby's second day of school, an adult woman threatened to poison her. On another day, a woman stood along Ruby's route to school displaying a Black doll in a wooden coffin.[2] Ruby's family was threatened too.

As the story of what Ruby was doing in Louisiana became better known, Robert Coles traveled to New Orleans to meet her. He wanted to understand how a little girl could do what she was doing, and he was concerned that she would be profoundly psychologically harmed by what she was enduring. Coles spent hours with Ruby, trying to help her, all while he was studying and learning from her.

Coles recounts, "Still, Ruby persisted, and so did her parents." He writes that Ruby "appeared strong, but she would soon enough show signs of psychological wear and tear." Coles considered a number of theories for why Ruby was acting in the way she was, theories of "denying" and "reaction formation."[3]

At one point, though, Coles came upon an interesting bit of information from one of the teachers at the school, who reported on this scene:

> I was standing in the classroom, looking out the window, and I saw Ruby coming down the street, with the federal marshals on both sides of her. The crowd was there, shouting, as usual. A woman spat at Ruby but missed, Ruby smiled at her. A man shook his fist at her; Ruby smiled at him. Then she walked up the stairs, and she stopped and turned around and smiled one more time! You know what she told one of the marshals? She told him she prays for those people, the ones in that mob, every night before she goes to sleep![4]

Coles had to follow up on this! He had been interested in how Ruby slept as an indicator of her psychological state, but he hadn't thought to ask about what she did right before she slept. And so he asked her about her prayers. He recounts, "Ruby was cheerful and matter-of-fact, if terse, in her reply: 'Yes, I do pray for them.'" Coles asked her why, and she replied, "'Because.'"

He writes, "I waited for more but to no effect. I started over, told her I was curious about why she would want to pray for people who were so unswervingly nasty to her. 'I go to church,' she told me, 'every Sunday, and we're told to pray for everyone, even the bad people, and so I do.' She had no more to say on that score."[5]

Coles continues,

> When I finally began to take notice of Ruby's churchgoing activities, and those of her parents, I'm afraid I was not very responsive to what I heard and saw. I kept wanting to fit what I was learning into what I had already learned . . . in order to say yes once more to the psychological theory I'd acquired before going South. Ruby was picking up phrases, admonitions, statements ritually expressed, bits and pieces of sermons emotionally delivered, and using all that in a gesture of obedience. She was being psychologically imitative. . . . She did what she was told, but did she truly understand what she was doing? Was she not, rather, showing herself to be a particular six-year-old child: scared, vulnerable . . . limited cognitively . . . grasping at whatever straws came her way?[6]

Coles continued to press Ruby so he could continue with his analysis. She told him, "They keep coming and saying the bad words, but my momma says they'll get tired after a while and then they'll stop coming. They'll stay home. The minister came to our house and he said the same thing, and not to worry, and I don't. The minister said God is watching and He won't forget, because He never does. The minister says if I forgive the people, and smile at them and pray for them, God will keep a good eye on everything and He'll be our protection."[7]

Coles thought he sensed doubt in Ruby's voice, and so he asked her if she believed the minister. She replied, "Oh, yes . . . I'm sure God knows what's happening. He's got a lot to worry about; but there is bad trouble here, and He can't help but notice. He may not rush to do anything, not right away. But there will come a day, like you hear in church."[8]

Coles continued his psychological analysis but couldn't make much headway with his existing theories. His wife, Coles writes, was skeptical, but not toward Ruby Bridges and her family, but "at the kind of inquiry I seemed determined to make. The more I tried to understand the emotional conflicts, the tensions and responses to tensions, the underlying motivations, and the projections and displacements; the more I emphasized the automatic or reflexive behavior of the children we knew, a consequence of their short lives, their lack of education, their limited cognitive development, their inability to handle all sorts of concepts and symbols; the more I read and commented on various developmental points of view, which emphasized stages and phases and periods . . . the more my wife kept pointing to the *acts* of these boys and girls, the *deeds* they managed."[9]

RUBY BRIDGES'S PRESUMPTION

I've had the opportunity to teach several classes of college students about Ruby Bridges's story. They hear about what Ruby did. They read, even, of Robert Coles coming to terms with Ruby's own testimony. Yet many of the students insist that what she did is impossible and unthinkable. If Ruby were older, she would have understood that you don't put yourself in danger's way like that. If she had been more mature, she would have realized that some people just should not be prayed for, but rather condemned. Six-year-old Ruby said some nice things, the kind of things Christians are supposed to say, but do we treat these "platitudes" as reality? Maybe it would be nice to act that way, but there's no conceivable way to get there. What she did—it makes no sense. These are the things that students of various faith backgrounds, including Christians, have said.

And yet Ruby Bridges *did* do those things. She said what she said, and she did what she did. Ruby's actions, not just the "what" but the "how," poured forth from her heart and affected everyone around her.

Her family and her church were witnesses to her faithfulness. Her courage to walk through those crowds of hateful people made it possible for other Black boys and girls in her neighborhood and city to attend integrated schools. Across the nation, activists and common, ordinary, everyday folks saw what she was doing and took inspiration from it.

Not everything was solved, of course. Some of those who cursed Ruby likely never repented. Many White families fled to the suburbs rather than place their children in an integrated school. Louisiana continued to put up roadblocks to fair school integration and educational equity.[10] But Ruby made a difference. And not only in her own time, but for ours.

When I think of Ruby Bridges, I think of a Norman Rockwell painting of her titled *The Problem We All Live With*. The painting depicts little Ruby in a white dress with a bow in her hair, carrying school supplies. She's marching, surrounded by four federal marshals. On the wall behind her is a graffitied racial epithet and the letters KKK etched into the wall, with the remains of a thrown tomato on the sidewalk alongside the wall.

I think of this painting because when I worked in the White House, the painting was displayed right outside of the Oval Office. I would walk by it on my way to the Roosevelt Room or the Oval. Sometimes if had a moment of quiet, I walked over just to look at it. Others, too, were moved by the painting. If you were going to meet with the president, you might be seated outside of the Oval before it was your turn to go in and you'd look at little Ruby.

Everyone who meets with the president has something burning in their heart that they want to say, that they think is important, but even the boldest can wilt under the pressure. The Oval Office is intimidating. The presidency can be intimidating.

But I know stories of people who, as they felt the pressure, unsure of themselves and their qualifications to do what they had been called to do, what people were counting on them to do, looked at Ruby Bridges and thought, *If she could do what she did, certainly I can have the courage to stand for what I believe is right.*

Imagine that. The faithfulness of six-year-old Ruby Bridges inspired adults fifty years later who had an audience with the president to advocate for their vision of the public good.

A CHILDLIKE FAITH

Dallas Willard was once asked whether the title of the final chapter of his book *Knowing Christ Today*—"Pastors as Teachers of the Nations"—could come across as presumptuous. He responded, as I noted earlier in this book, "That is exactly right. Jesus is the most presumptuous person who ever lived."[11] He explained further:

> Jesus' effect on people was different from that of the scribes and Pharisees. That was because he spoke as one having authority, and people noticed that. . . . The amazing thing about Jesus—and I hope you might look carefully at the logic

of his words—was how he was able to refer to reality and cause people to understand it in a different way. Usually it was in a way that got past the hardened traditions of those people who thought they were in charge of the religious life. The test of religious life is life, and that is where Jesus lived it. And that's why he refers to children and says that if you are going to enter the kingdom of God, you have to become like a little child. Now, apart from Jesus, the next most presumptuous person in the world is a little child. They just go, you know. The main thing is, when you hear Jesus, do what he says. Don't build a theory. Just do what he says, and reality will teach you, and that is where authority ultimately lies. So the test for the secularist and the Christian spokesperson is the reality that they bring people in touch with.[12]

Ruby Bridges put into practice what Jesus said, as well as the knowledge about Jesus that she had learned from her parents and pastor. Given our tendency to presume on our politics, what might change if we were to presume only on Jesus and his promises in our political behavior and posture?

CIVIC PARTICIPATION

If we were a different kind of people, we would see an explosion of positive, constructive civic participation. Less energy would be directed toward frivolous entertainment, and people would look for ways in which their passions, knowledge, and experiences could be of service. More people would run for local office, and there would be greater interest in local politics. Leaders would rise up with particular insight on certain aspects of government because people would be looking for partners in the project of self-governance. We'd see a resurgence of public meetings, community organizations, civic education efforts, and local civic philanthropy. There would be a rise in democratic innovation as we created new ways to empower citizens to speak into political processes. We would make it easier for people to vote, and more people would vote, but we would understand that the vote is the baseline of our democratic expression, not the height of it.

People would view political parties as vehicles for political action, not as primary sources of identity. Political parties would lose their ability to dictate citizens' ideas and instead be shaped by citizens. Party affiliation would no longer be a signal of personal character because we would have a number of political parties all constructed around positive visions for social good.

Politics would be one area of life in which we seek social improvement, but it wouldn't be the only, or even the primary, one. The burden on politics would be lifted because people would be looking out for one another outside of politics. Our values would run both ways. We would apply our personal values to our political life but also our political values to our personal lives. Volunteerism would rise. Donations to charities would rise. The strength of our social ties would spur a healthier politics, and a healthier politics would restore social trust and promote social cohesion.

FROM ILL WILL TO GOODWILL

If we were a different kind of people, fewer women and men would go to politics seeking to act out their resentments, and we'd see ill will gradually diminish in our political discourse.

The desire to do harm through our politics would be strongly disincentivized because it would repel voters rather than attract them. We would have less of a punitive impulse and be less likely to seek revenge in our personal lives, and our politics would increasingly take on that character. Instead of bad-faith arguments and character assassination, our politics would display forgiveness, mercy, gentleness, compassion, truth, beauty, grace, love, and other expressions of moral goodness.

Our political culture, resourced by the character of the citizens contributing to it, would inspire and support a broader culture of goodwill. Instead of politics dividing churches and families, political participation would train people to negotiate with one another and address competing interests in more personal circumstances. In politics, community exchanges, church life, family life, personal and romantic relationships, and our own thought lives, we would be far more oriented toward willing the good for others rather than seeking their harm.

THE POOR AND DISINHERITED

If we were a different kind of people, the poor and disinherited would receive special preference in our attention, not scorn. No longer dominated by our own self-interest or a politics of entertainment and resentment, we would carry with us the interests of the least of these as we voted, advocated, and even discussed politics. Our first instinct would not be to pathologize or lecture people in poverty, but rather to improve their station. Politics would not be the only area of life in which this was done, but it wouldn't be excluded either.

Poverty, both domestic and global, would plummet. Homelessness would decrease. Maternal and infant mortality rates would go down. Economic inequality would narrow. Workers would be protected. The elderly would be cared for and valued.

Injustice would not be exploited for self-aggrandizement, and the poor would not be pawns in a game played by elites. We would take justice too seriously to use injustice to justify further injustice.

We would take significant pride in our government's efforts to address poverty and injustice because we would have contributed to them. Programs like the US President's Emergency Plan for AIDS Relief would be considered part of our national history of achievements, a statement of who we are as a people, joining with our stories of industrial and military achievement.[13]

ORDER

Dallas Willard once wrote, "The Ten Commandments given to Moses are so deep and powerful on these matters that if humanity followed them, daily life would be transformed beyond recognition and large segments of the public media would collapse for lack of material. Consider a daily newspaper or television newscast, and eliminate from it every report that presupposes a breaking of one of the Ten Commandments. Very little will be left."[14]

This is undeniably true, and if we were to make progress in becoming the kind of people we are called to be, in living the kind of life Jesus offers, it would be true for us. Crime of all kinds would go down. Our legal system would be less burdened and run more effectively. Family life would be extraordinarily generative and serve as a foundation for stronger and more resilient communities. Social trust would skyrocket. And all of this would lead to a healthier politics, capable of promoting even greater flourishing.

IS IT POSSIBLE?

It seems improbable now, with our politics as sick as it is, our illusions dispelled and our plans thwarted. The old political answers that once captivated our attention now seem inadequate. There is such disappointment. It can feel like we have reached our end. What future is there for our politics? For our churches? For us? When will our politics provide us with the right answers?

It is there, at our end, that we find a new beginning. What if we stopped contorting ourselves to fit a politics that is not serving us? What if we stopped taking our cues from a politics that makes us so small? Our politics has no answers it does not first receive from us. At the center of our faith is not a series of right answers, but a person. This is what we have to offer our politics: the kind of person we are. If you want to change our politics, this is where you will start.

It really is the answer hiding in plain sight. If we want a better politics, we need to become a different kind of people. It won't be easy. Political change won't be immediate. It will require us to catch a vision, form an intention to live into that vision, and take up the means to follow through. Instead of seeking a magic solution, the program or ideology that will fix all our social ills without us ever having to actually become anything different, this vision recognizes that democratic solutions are contingent on those who make up the democracy.

We also understand the limitations of politics. "The greatest temptation to evil that human ever suffers is the temptation to make a 'Jerusalem' happen by human means," Willard warns. "Human means are absolutely indispensable in the world as it is. That is God's intention. We are supposed to act, and our actions are to count. But there is a limit on what human arrangements can accomplish. They alone cannot change the heart and spirit of the human being."[15] Our politics needs this knowledge as well. We should be chastened by it. Our actions in politics are to count, but neither heaven nor hell hinges on a vote or a policy.

We must take responsibility for who we are as Christians and what we have to offer as citizens. "The world can no longer be left to mere diplomats, politicians, and business leaders," wrote Dallas Willard. "They have done the best they could, no doubt. But this is an age for spiritual heroes—a time for men and women to be heroic in faith and in spiritual character and power."[16]

I have seen our politics up close. I've briefed a president in the Oval Office. I've been a participant in our political and public life for nearly two decades. I've seen communities change and lives made better because of politics, just as I've seen the opposite. What I can promise you is that it is people who make the difference, and it does not take many people acting differently to make a difference in our politics and in people's lives. Spiritual formation is central to civic renewal.

OUR FINAL AIM

Yet if our vision only extends as far as a better politics, an improved society, a flourishing world, we will be aiming too low. There is something more. There is a greater horizon to which we look.

"We are, all of us, never-ceasing spiritual beings with a unique eternal calling to count for good in God's great universe," Willard wrote.[17] "The purpose of God with human history is nothing less than to bring out of it—small and insignificant as it seems from the biological and naturalistic point of view—an eternal community of those who were once thought to be just 'ordinary human beings.' Because of God's purposes for it, this community will, in its way, pervade the entire created realm and share in the government of it. God's precreation intention to have that community as a special dwelling place or home will be realized. He will be its prime sustainer and most glorious inhabitant."[18]

It is with this bright future in mind that we begin now to do our part to place all that we have a say in under the jurisdiction of love. We live in the light of that vision.

This future unfolds before us even now. It does not begin at some later date. You are living this story at this very moment. This is not doctrine or tradition or argument, but life—*your life*. We are learning now to make heaven our home, and as we are saturated by the love of God, heaven makes its home with us.

Then, as God will have it, the earth will be as the heavens and love will finally retake its place at the center of human affairs.

The throne of God and of the Lamb will be in the city, and his servants will serve him. They will see his face, and his name will be on their foreheads. There will be no more night. They will not need the light of a lamp or the light of the sun, for the Lord God will give them light. And they will reign for ever and ever. (Revelation 22:3–5)

ACKNOWLEDGMENTS

This book would have been impossible without some specific people.

I never knew Dallas Willard personally, but I am so grateful for all that his work and example have meant in my life. Thank you to the Willard family, especially Becky, for your support and encouragement.

Gary Haugen sent *The Divine Conspiracy* to my office when I was a twenty-year-old White House staffer, and my first pastor, Jerry Gillis, convinced me to read Willard for the first time. What a tremendous gift!

Webb Younce, the editor of this book and my first book, *Reclaiming Hope*, made this book possible. I am thankful for your wisdom and partnership.

Thank you to the entire team at Zondervan, including Katie Painter, Devin Duke, Dirk Buursma, Paul Fisher, and Matt Bray. You are all so good at your jobs, and you are such wonderful people.

James Catford, my friend and the founding chair of the Center for Christianity and Public Life (CCPL), thank you for your confidence in me. I am glad and honored to be one of your "boys out there."

Thank you to those who provided invaluable research or feedback that informed this book, including Phebe Meyer, Joy Harris, Chris Crawford, Caroline Kopsky, Steve Porter, Brandon Rickabough, John Inazu, Andy Crouch, Tish Harrison Warren, Samuel Kimbriel, John Ortberg, and Laura Turner.

I am tremendously grateful for the Perry family; the Kling family; the Reyes family; Revd Professor David Wilkinson and St. John's College, Durham, UK; and Steven Purcell and the Laity Lodge. All of these individuals and institutions provided a hospitable and generative place for me to work on this book at critical points in the writing process. Thank you to all of you!

The ideas in this book are at the heart of CCPL, and so I am profoundly grateful for CCPL's board of directors and staff, financial supporters, programmatic partners, and those we serve.

Melissa, my partner in all and the one who has all of my love, thank you for all you do and all you bear for our good and our family's good. You read this book so many times. You are my favorite possibility.

Praise God from whom all blessings flow.

NOTES

Introduction

1. See Eli J. Finkel et al., "Political Sectarianism in America: A Poisonous Cocktail of Othering, Aversion, and Moralization Poses a Threat to Democracy," *Science* 370, no. 6516 (October 2020): 533–36, https://lskitka.people.uic.edu/Sectarianism.pdf.
2. See Deborah Netburn, "Feeling Anxious about the Election? Here's How to Cope with Election Stress Disorder," *Los Angeles Times*, November 4, 2016, www.latimes.com/science/sciencenow/la-sci-sn-election-stress-disorder-20161104-story.html.
3. See Anna Merod, "Report: Children of Color 'Terrified' of Trump Presidency," MSNBC, April 14, 2016, www.msnbc.com/msnbc/report-children-color-terrified-about-trump-presidency-msna832376.
4. I'm grateful for Gary Moon's biography of Dallas Willard, which has informed this section and my understanding of who Dallas Willard was as a person. See Gary Moon, *Becoming Dallas Willard: The Formation of a Philosopher, Teacher, and Christ Follower* (Downers Grove, IL: InterVarsity, 2018).
5. Dallas Willard, *The Great Omission: Reclaiming Jesus's Essential Teachings on Discipleship* (San Francisco: HarperSanFrancisco, 2006), xiv.

Chapter 1: Our Political Sickness

1. See "Public Trust in Government: 1958–2022," Pew Research Center, June 6, 2022, www.pewresearch.org/politics/2022/06/06/public-trust-in-government-1958-2022.

2. See "Americans' Views of Government: Decades of Distrust, Enduring Support for Its Role," Pew Research Center, June 6, 2022, www.pewresearch.org/politics/2022/06/06/americans-views-of -government-decades-of-distrust-enduring-support-for-its-role.

3. See Eli J. Finkel et al., "Political Sectarianism in America: A Poisonous Cocktail of Othering, Aversion, and Moralization Poses a Threat to Democracy," *Science* 370, no. 6516 (October 2020): 533–36, https://lskitka.people.uic.edu/Sectarianism.pdf.

4. Finkel, "Political Sectarianism."

5. Finkel, "Political Sectarianism."

6. Finkel, "Political Sectarianism."

7. Finkel, "Political Sectarianism."

8. Finkel, "Political Sectarianism."

9. Matthew H. Graham and Milan W. Svolik, "Democracy in America? Partisanship, Polarization, and the Robustness of Support for Democracy in the United States," *American Political Science Review* 114, no. 2 (May 2020): 392–409, www.cambridge.org/core/journals/american -political-science-review/article/abs/democracy-in-america-partisanship -polarization-and-the-robustness-of-support-for-democracy-in-the -united-states/C7C72745B1AD1FF9E363BBFBA9E18867.

10. Mike Cummings, "Study: Americans Prize Party Loyalty over Democratic Principles," YaleNews, August 11, 2020, https://news .yale.edu/2020/08/11/study-americans-prize-party-loyalty-over -democratic-principles, italics added.

11. For a more extended version of this argument, see my chapter, "Christian and Democrat," in *Cultural Engagement*, ed. Joshua D. Chatraw and Karen Swallow Prior (Grand Rapids: Zondervan Academic, 2019), 239–45.

12. Catie Edmondson, "With Name-Calling and Twitter Battles, House Republican Campaign Arm Copies Trump's Playbook," *New York Times*, July 17, 2019, www.nytimes.com/2019/07/17/us/politics/donald -trump-republicans.html.

13. Matthew Rosenberg and Kevin Roose, "Trump Campaign Floods Web with Ads, Raking in Cash as Democrats Struggle," *New York Times*, October 20, 2019, www.nytimes.com/2019/10/20/us/elections /trump-campaign-ads-democrats.html.

14. See Stephen Hawkins et al., "Hidden Tribes: A Study of America's

Polarized Landscape," More in Common, 2018, https://hiddentribes
.us/media/qfpekz4g/hidden_tribes_report.pdf.

15. Eitan Hersh, "College-Educated Voters Are Ruining American Politics," *The Atlantic*, January 20, 2020, www.theatlantic.com/ideas /archive/2020/01/political-hobbyists-are-ruining-politics/605212.

16. Sean Illing, "Why Liberals Are Bad at Politics," *Vox*, March 1, 2020, www.vox.com/policy-and-politics/2020/2/18/21112012/liberals -conservatives-american-politics-eitan-hersh.

17. Jon Askonas provides extraordinary insight into this point in his essay "How Stewart Made Tucker," *New Atlantis*, October 5, 2022, www.thenewatlantis.com/publications/how-stewart-made-tucker.

18. Quoted in Illing, "Why Liberals Are Bad at Politics."

19. Eitan Hersh, *Politics Is for Power: How to Move beyond Political Hobbyism, Take Action, and Make Real Change* (New York: Scribner, 2020), 4.

20. Hersh, *Politics Is for Power*, 5.

21. The seventh tribe, Traditional Conservatives, is part of the "wings" of the electorate, along with Progressive Activists and Devoted Conservatives, because they "tend to hold views that conform to their tribe and do not deviate from the party line."

22. Christian Smith with Melinda Lundquist Denton, *Soul Searching: The Religious and Spiritual Lives of American Teenagers* (New York: Oxford University Press, 2005).

23. An instructive excerpt from an interview with Dr. Smith: "Well, first, MTD [moralistic therapeutic deism] is not Christianity. It's a different religion. So if youth raised in Christian homes (and their parents!) think that MTD is Christianity, then they can assume that they are good Christians and not worry anymore. What pastors say can float right over their heads, which very often happens. The challenge is getting people to see the contrast between MTD and real Christianity, without being negative, condemning, defensive, sectarian, etc." (Chris Martin, "It's Complicated: An Interview with Dr. Christian Smith," Millennial Evangelical, August 16, 2016).

24. Quoted in Dallas Willard, "Connecting with Reality," Renovaré Institute, October 15, 2010, https://conversatio.org/connecting-with -reality.

25. This idea is discussed in my previous book, *Reclaiming Hope: Lessons*

Learned in the Obama White House about the Future of Faith in America (Nashville: Nelson, 2018).

26. See Ryan Burge, "Why 'Evangelical' Is Becoming Another Word for 'Republican,'" *New York Times*, October 26, 2021, www.nytimes.com /2021/10/26/opinion/evangelical-republican.html.

27. See Michele F. Margolis, *From Politics to the Pews: How Partisanship and the Political Environment Shape Religious Identity* (Chicago: University of Chicago Press, 2018).

28. Tim Alberta, "How Politics Poisoned the Evangelical Church," *The Atlantic*, May 10, 2022, www.theatlantic.com/magazine/archive/2022 /06/evangelical-church-pastors-political-radicalization/629631.

Chapter 2: The Disappearance of Moral Knowledge

1. See Philip Bump, "Tucker Carlson's Disingenuous Effort to Exonerate the 'QAnon Shaman,'" *Washington Post*, March 13, 2023, www .washingtonpost.com/politics/2023/03/13/tucker-carlson-jan6 -insurrection-qanon-shaman.

2. Luke Mogelson, "Among the Insurrectionists," *New Yorker*, January 25, 2021, www.newyorker.com/magazine/2021/01/25/among -the-insurrectionists.

3. See "Religious Freedom Index: American Perspectives on the First Amendment, 4th ed.," Becket, December 2022, https://becketnewsite .s3.amazonaws.com/20221207155617/Religious-Freedom-Index-2022 .pdf.

4. See Tom Holland, *Dominion: How the Christian Revolution Remade the World* (New York: Basic Books, 2019); Rodney Stark, *America's Blessings: How Religion Benefits Everyone, Including Atheists* (Conshohocken, PA: Templeton Press, 2012).

5. Dallas Willard, *The Disappearance of Moral Knowledge* (New York: Routledge, 2018), xxx, italics in original.

6. Willard, *Disappearance of Moral Knowledge*, xxx, italics in original.

7. Willard, *Disappearance of Moral Knowledge*, 8.

8. Willard, *Disappearance of Moral Knowledge*, 9–10.

9. Willard, *Disappearance of Moral Knowledge*, 10–11.

10. Willard, *Disappearance of Moral Knowledge*, 11–12.

11. See Willard, *Disappearance of Moral Knowledge*, 13.

12. Willard, *Disappearance of Moral Knowledge*, 14, italics in original.

13. Willard, *Disappearance of Moral Knowledge*, 14, italics in original.
14. Dallas Willard, *The Divine Conspiracy: Rediscovering Our Hidden Life in God* (San Francisco: HarperSanFrancisco, 1998), 3–4.
15. Robert Coles, "The Disparity between Intellect and Character," *Chronicle of Higher Education*, September 22, 1995, www.chronicle.com/article/the-disparity-between-intellect-and-character.
16. Coles, "Disparity between Intellect and Character."
17. Coles, "Disparity between Intellect and Character."
18. Willard, *Divine Conspiracy*, 4.
19. Willard, *Divine Conspiracy*, 4–5, italics in original.
20. Dallas Willard, *Knowing Christ Today: Why We Can Trust Spiritual Knowledge* (San Francisco: HarperSanFrancisco, 2009), 71, italics in original.
21. Christine Emba, *Rethinking Sex: A Provocation* (New York: Sentinel, 2022).
22. G. K. Chesterton, *Orthodoxy* (New York: Image Books, 1959), 27.
23. See John F. Kennedy, "Address of Senator John F. Kennedy to the Greater Houston Ministerial Association, September 12, 1960," Rice Hotel, Houston, Texas, September 12, 1960, www.jfklibrary.org/archives/other-resources/john-f-kennedy-speeches/houston-tx-19600912-houston-ministerial-association.
24. Willard, *Knowing Christ Today*, 30–31, italics in original.
25. Willard, *Knowing Christ Today*, 32.
26. Willard, *Knowing Christ Today*, 25.
27. See Justin Welby, "The Archbishop of Canterbury's Sermon for the State Funeral of Her Majesty Queen Elizabeth II," Westminster Abbey, London, England, September 19, 2022, www.archbishopofcanterbury.org/speaking-writing/sermons/archbishop-canterburys-sermon-state-funeral-her-majesty-queen-elizabeth-ii.
28. Caroline Davies, "King Tells Faith Leaders He Has Personal 'Duty to Protect Diversity of Our Country,'" *The Guardian*, September 16, 2022, www.theguardian.com/uk-news/2022/sep/16/king-tells-faith-leaders-he-has-personal-duty-to-protect-diversity-of-our-country.
29. Justin Welby, "Archbishop of Canterbury's Speech on Shared National Values," House of Lords debate, London, England, December 12, 2016, www.churchofengland.org/news-and-media/news-and-statements/archbishop-canterburys-speech-shared-national-values.

30. See Kristen O'Neill, "'Multiple Ways of Knowing': Advancing Indigenous Perspectives to Elevate Science, Communities," University of Colorado Anschutz Medical Campus, October 12, 2020, https:// news.cuanschutz.edu/news-stories/multiple-ways-of-knowing -advancing-indigenous-perspectives-to-elevate-science-communities.

31. Clément Desmouceaux et al., "In Sickness and in Health: How Health Is Perceived around the World," McKinsey Health Institute, July 21, 2022, www.mckinsey.com/mhi/our-insights/in-sickness-and-in -health-how-health-is-perceived-around-the-world.

32. See, for example, "Center for Spirituality, Theology and Health," Duke University, https://spiritualityandhealth.duke.edu, accessed April 17, 2023.

33. See Nellie Bowles, "These Millennials Got New Roommates. They're Nuns," *New York Times*, May 31, 2019, www.nytimes.com/2019/05/31 /style/milliennial-nuns-spiritual-quest.html.

Chapter 3: Gospels of Sin Management and Our Politics

1. For more on Christian ethics as good news, see Oliver O'Donovan, *Resurrection and Moral Order: An Outline for Evangelical Ethics*, 2nd ed. (Grand Rapids: Eerdmans, 1994).

2. Dallas Willard, *Living in Christ's Presence: Final Words on Heaven and the Kingdom of God* (Downers Grove, IL: InterVarsity, 2014), 10.

3. Dallas Willard, *The Divine Conspiracy* (San Francisco: HarperSanFrancisco, 1998), 36–37.

4. Willard, *Divine Conspiracy*, 49. "Anyone who thinks he or she does fully understand what theology calls the atonement undoubtedly has some surprises coming. Nowhere, I think, is theological arrogance more commonly displayed than on this subject" (*Divine Conspiracy*, 334).

5. Willard, *Divine Conspiracy*, 47.

6. Albert Mohler, "Moralism Is Not the Gospel (But Many Christians Think It Is)," AlbertMohler.com, April 8, 2014, https://albertmohler .com/2014/04/08/moralism-is-not-the-gospel-but-many-christians -think-it-is.

7. Tim Alberta, "Donald Trump Is on the Wrong Side of the Religious Right," *The Atlantic*, March 24, 2023, www.theatlantic.com/politics

/archive/2023/03/trump-religious-right-evangelical-vote-pence
-desantis-support/673475.

8. Quoted in Brandon Porter, "Mohler Addresses 'Fairy Tale' of
   Secular State, Calls Voting a 'Powerful Stewardship,'" *Baptist Press*,
   September 16, 2022, www.baptistpress.com/resource-library/news
   /mohler-addresses-fairy-tale-of-secular-state-calls-voting-a-powerful
   -stewardship.

9. Albert Mohler, Twitter post, September 15, 2022, 7:41 p.m., https://
   twitter.com/albertmohler/status/1570558362496159744.

10. "About," AlbertMohler.com, https://albertmohler.com/about; see
    "The Briefing," AlbertMohler.com, https://albertmohler.com/the
    -briefing, accessed April 20, 2023.

11. "Search: The Briefing," AlbertMohler.com, https://albertmohler.com
    /search/q/preselect+the-briefing/p/1, accessed April 20, 2023.

12. John MacArthur, interview with Ryan Helfenbein, "Church Is
    Essential w/Pastor John MacArthur | Give Me Liberty Ep. 58," Radio
    Public, August 12, 2020, https://radiopublic.com/give-me-liberty-with
    -ryan-helfenb-WzVeRE/s1!8ead7.

13. Albert Mohler, "By Failing to Address America's Astronomical
    National Debt, We Are Stealing from the Next Generation," The
    Briefing: Part I, October 27, 2016, https://albertmohler.com/2016/10
    /27/briefing-10-27-16.

14. See Tom Norton, "Fact Check: Was 40 Percent of National Debt
    'Accumulated' under Trump?" *Newsweek*, May 4, 2023, www
    .newsweek.com/donald-trump-debt-joe-biden-kevin-mccarthy
    -ceiling-1802049.

15. Willard, *Divine Conspiracy*, 51.

16. Willard, *Divine Conspiracy*, 53, italics in original.

17. Premier Journalist, "Hundreds Arrested at Faith-Focused Protest
    Near Capitol," Premier Christian News, August 3, 2021, https://
    premierchristian.news/us/news/article/hundreds-arrested-at-faith
    -focused-protest-near-capitol.

18. One striking feature of these interviews when taken as a whole is
    that Nicholas Kristof never appeared to actually process any of the
    answers he received. There was no sense in which the interviews
    built from one or the other. Though he returns over and over to his
    admiration of and respect for Jesus' teachings, he doesn't show any

appreciation for the ways in which Jesus' teachings invoke and rely on the "miracles."

19. I particularly like the spirit and content of Cardinal Joseph Tobin's answer to a similar answer from Kristof: "People are, I guess, free to take whatever they want. Just like there's wisdom in non-Christian religions that Christians appropriate. The most mind-boggling miracle is the incarnation. We believe that the Creator of the Universe, the one who existed before time and before anything else, became one of us. If you accept that, then there are a lot of other things that don't seem to be quite as unbelievable" (Nicholas Kristof, "Cardinal Tobin, Am I a Christian?" *New York Times*, www.nytimes .com/2017/12/22/opinion/sunday/cardinal-tobin-christian.html).

20. Here again I wish to emphasize that I do not mention Dr. Jones to criticize her personally. In fact, she is a friend, and I have spoken at her institution by her invitation. As with Al Mohler, I have personally benefited from her work and leadership in some ways, even as I disagree with her in others.

21. Nicholas Kristof, "Reverend, You Say the Virgin Birth Is a 'Bizarre Claim'?" *New York Times*, April 20, 2019, www.nytimes.com/2019/04 /20/opinion/sunday/christian-easter-serene-jones.html.

22. Willard, *Divine Conspiracy*, 54.

23. Dallas Willard, *The Great Omission: Reclaiming Jesus's Essential Teachings on Discipleship* (San Francisco: HarperSanFrancisco, 2006), x–xi.

Chapter 4: Kingdom Politics

1. A. W. Tozer, *The Knowledge of the Holy* (New York: Harper & Row, 1978), 1.

2. Dallas Willard, *The Divine Conspiracy: Rediscovering Our Hidden Life in God* (San Francisco: HarperSanFrancisco, 1998), 62.

3. Willard, *Divine Conspiracy*, 63, italics in original.

4. Willard, *Divine Conspiracy*, 64.

5. Dallas Willard, *Living in Christ's Presence: Final Words on Heaven and the Kingdom of God* (Downers Grove, IL: InterVarsity, 2014), 34.

6. "Dallas Willard—God Wants to Be Seen," Episode 184, *Renovaré Podcast* with Nathan Foster, May 4, 2020, https://share.transistor.fm/s /a4e57a74.

7. Willard, *Divine Conspiracy*, 66, italics in original.

8. Dallas Willard, *The Allure of Gentleness: Defending the Faith in the Manner of Jesus* (San Francisco: HarperOne, 2015), 27.

9. Dallas Willard, *The Great Omission: Reclaiming Jesus's Essential Teachings on Discipleship* (San Francisco: HarperSanFrancisco, 2006), xi.

10. Willard, *Divine Conspiracy*, 27.

11. Willard, *Allure of Gentleness*, 20.

12. Willard, *Divine Conspiracy*, 25, italics in original.

13. Willard, *Divine Conspiracy*, 25.

14. Willard, *Divine Conspiracy*, 25.

15. Willard, *Living in Christ's Presence*, 25.

16. See Willard, *Divine Conspiracy*, 73–75.

17. Willard, *Divine Conspiracy*, 25.

18. Willard, *Divine Conspiracy*, 100, italics in original.

19. Willard, *Divine Conspiracy*, 102, italics in original.

20. Willard, *Divine Conspiracy*, 123.

21. Willard, *Divine Conspiracy*, 283.

22. Willard, *Divine Conspiracy*, 24.

23. Dallas Willard, *Knowing Christ Today: Why We Can Trust Spiritual Knowledge* (San Francisco: HarperOne, 2009), 83, italics in original.

24. C. S. Lewis, *Mere Christianity* (New York: Macmillan, 1960), 78–79.

25. The majority of the content in this section comes from a post based on my remarks at an event hosted by Coracle, a nonprofit ministry offering spiritual formation and kingdom action. See "How Christians Should Think about Voting," Wear We Are, October 10, 2020, https://wearweare.substack.com/p/how-christians-should-think-about.

26. Parker J. Palmer, "The Politics of the Brokenhearted," in *Healing the Heart of Democracy* (San Francisco: Jossey-Bass, 2011), 1–10, https://couragerenewal.org/wp-content/uploads/2022/06/Parker-Palmer_politicsbrokenhearted.pdf.

Chapter 5: The Allure of Gentleness: Christian Politics as Loving Service

1. Dallas Willard, *The Allure of Gentleness: Defending the Faith in the Manner of Jesus* (San Francisco: HarperOne, 2015), 1–2.

2. Willard, *Allure of Gentleness*, 2, italics in original.

3. Willard, *Allure of Gentleness*, 46–47.

4. Willard, *Allure of Gentleness*, 47.

5. Willard, *Allure of Gentleness*, 47.

6. Willard, *Allure of Gentleness*, 49.

7. See Willard, *Allure of Gentleness*, 49–50.

8. Willard, *Allure of Gentleness*, 52.

9. Willard, *Allure of Gentleness*, 52.

10. Willard, *Allure of Gentleness*, 53.

11. Dallas Willard, *Knowing Christ Today: Why We Can Trust Spiritual Knowledge* (San Francisco: HarperOne, 2009), 155.

12. Willard, *Knowing Christ Today*, 171–72.

13. Michel Foucault, *"Society Must Be Defended": Lectures at the Collège de France* (New York: Picador, 1997), 15.

14. Dallas Willard, *The Divine Conspiracy: Rediscovering Our Hidden Life in God* (San Francisco: HarperSanFrancisco, 1998), 147, italics in original.

15. See "Anger Motivates People to Vote, U-M Study Shows," University of Michigan Institute for Social Research, June 7, 2011.

16. Augustine of Hippo, "Letter 38 (A.D. 397)," New Advent, www.newadvent.org/fathers/1102038.htm, accessed April 24, 2022.

17. Willard, *Divine Conspiracy*, 148.

18. See Howard Thurman, *Jesus and the Disinherited* (Boston: Beacon, 1976). See the discussion of Thurman's approach to hatred in Justin Giboney, Michael Wear, and Chris Butler, *Compassion (&) Conviction: The And Campaign's Guide to Faithful Civic Engagement* (Downers Grove, IL: InterVarsity, 2020) for an extended application of Thurman's views to our current political situation.

19. Willard, *Divine Conspiracy*, 151.

20. Willard, *Divine Conspiracy*, 152.

21. These kinds of justifications are offered in these two articles: Jessica Yarvin, "What the #$@! Democrats Are Swearing More. Here's Why," PBS News Hour, July 11, 2017, www.pbs.org/newshour/politics/democrats-swearing-heres; Judy Kurtz, "F-bombs Away: Why Lawmakers Are Cursing Now More Than Ever," The Hill, August 18, 2019, https://thehill.com/blogs/in-the-know/in-the-know/457732-f-bombs-away-why-lawmakers-are-cursing-now-more-than-ever/.

22. Willard, *Divine Conspiracy*, 151.

23. Augustine, "Letter 38 (A.D. 397)."

24. Willard, *Divine Conspiracy*, 151.

25. Willard, *Divine Conspiracy*, 84.
26. Amber A'Lee Frost, "The Necessity of Political Vulgarity," *Current Affairs*, August 25, 2016, www.currentaffairs.org/2016/08/the -necessity-of-political-vulgarity.
27. Again, this is why I am less sanguine than others about the wisdom and benefit of mobilizing the "Exhausted Majority." Perhaps it provides a new surge of political energy that is not consumed by toxic polarization and extremism. But it also seems possible that newly engaged citizens will be drafted into toxic polarization, particularly if they are not drawing on robust resources that will help them resist toxic modes of political participation.
28. This is one reason I caution against placing all hope for our politics in mobilizing the "Exhausted Majority."
29. I can't help but think of Sheldon Vanauken's *A Severe Mercy* and his "Shining Barrier" (San Francisco: HarperSanFrancisco, 1980), 36.
30. Dietrich Bonhoeffer, *Life Together* (New York: Harper & Row, 1954), 34
31. Bonhoeffer, *Life Together*, 34.
32. Bonhoeffer, *Life Together*, 35, italics added.
33. Willard, *Divine Conspiracy*, 236.
34. Bonhoeffer, *Life Together*, 35.
35. Bonhoeffer, *Life Together*, 36.
36. Bonhoeffer, *Life Together*, 36.

Chapter 6: The Kind of People We Are

1. Dallas Willard, *Renovation of the Heart: Putting on the Character of Christ* (Colorado Springs: NavPress, 2002), 19, italics in original.
2. "Dr. Martin Luther King Jr.'s Visit to WMU: Transcription of MLK's WMU Speech," Western Michigan University Libraries, December 18, 1963, https://libguides.wmich.edu/mlkatwmu/speech.
3. "Dr. Martin Luther King Jr.'s Visit to WMU."
4. C. S. Lewis, *Mere Christianity* (New York: Macmillan, 1960), 82–83.
5. Willard, *Renovation of the Heart*, 15.
6. Willard, *Renovation of the Heart*, 22, italics in original.
7. Willard, *Renovation of the Heart*, 22.
8. Dallas Willard, *The Divine Conspiracy: Rediscovering Our Hidden Life in God* (San Francisco: HarperSanFrancisco, 1998), 283, italics in original.
9. Willard, *Renovation of the Heart*, 32, italics in original.

10. Willard, *Renovation of the Heart*, 32.

11. Willard, *Renovation of the Heart*, 32–33.

12. Willard, *Renovation of the Heart*, 33, italics in original.

13. Willard, *Renovation of the Heart*, 34.

14. Willard, *Renovation of the Heart*, 34.

15. Willard, *Renovation of the Heart*, 35.

16. Willard, *Renovation of the Heart*, 36–37.

17. Willard, *Renovation of the Heart*, 37, italics in original.

18. Willard, *Renovation of the Heart*, 41–42.

19. Andy Crouch, *The Life We're Looking For: Reclaiming Relationship in a Technological World* (New York: Convergent, 2022), 60.

20. Crouch, *Life We're Looking For*, 60–61.

21. Crouch, *Life We're Looking For*, 66.

22. Crouch, *Life We're Looking For*, 78.

23. Willard, *Renovation of the Heart*, 85.

24. Willard, *Renovation of the Heart*, 85.

25. Willard, *Renovation of the Heart*, 85–86, italics in original.

26. Dallas Willard, *The Great Omission: Reclaiming Jesus's Essential Teachings on Discipleship* (San Francisco: HarperSanFrancisco, 2006), 100, italics in original.

27. James Catford, "End of the Year Reflection," Center for Christianity and Public Life, December 19, 2022, www.ccpubliclife.org/journal/blog-post-title-three-capha.

28. Willard, *Divine Conspiracy*, 218, italics in original.

29. Willard, *Divine Conspiracy*, 218.

30. Willard, *Divine Conspiracy*, 219.

31. Willard, *Divine Conspiracy*, 219, italics in original.

32. Willard, *Divine Conspiracy*, 219.

33. Willard, *Divine Conspiracy*, 129–30.

Chapter 7: Spiritual Disciplines for Public Life

1. Dallas Willard, *The Great Omission: Reclaiming Jesus's Essential Teachings on Discipleship* (San Francisco: HarperSanFrancisco, 2006), xiv, italics in original.

2. Dallas Willard, *Renovation of the Heart: Putting On the Character of Christ* (Colorado Springs: NavPress, 2002), 90, italics in original.

3. Dallas Willard, *The Divine Conspiracy: Rediscovering Our Hidden Life in God* (San Francisco: HarperSanFrancisco, 1998), 353.

4. Willard, *Divine Conspiracy*, 353.

5. Dallas Willard, *The Spirit of the Disciplines: Understanding How God Changes Lives* (San Francisco: HarperSanFrancisco, 1988), 160.

6. Willard, *Spirit of the Disciplines*, 176.

7. Willard, *Spirit of the Disciplines*, 176.

8. Willard, *Divine Conspiracy*, 364, italics in original.

9. Willard, *Spirit of the Disciplines*, 182.

10. Willard, *Spirit of the Disciplines*, 182.

11. Eli J. Finkel et al., "Political Sectarianism in America: A Poisonous Cocktail of Othering, Aversion, and Moralization Poses a Threat to Democracy," *Science* 370, no. 6516 (October 2020): 533–36, https://lskitka.people.uic.edu/Sectarianism.pdf.

12. Finkel, "Political Sectarianism in America."

13. Willard, *Divine Conspiracy*, 64, italics in original.

14. Willard, *Spirit of the Disciplines*, 160.

15. Willard, *Spirit of the Disciplines*, 160.

16. Willard, *Spirit of the Disciplines*, 172.

17. Willard, *Spirit of the Disciplines*, 172.

18. Willard, *Spirit of the Disciplines*, 176.

19. Willard, *Spirit of the Disciplines*, 176.

20. Willard, *Spirit of the Disciplines*, 177.

21. Willard, *Spirit of the Disciplines*, 177.

22. Willard, *Spirit of the Disciplines*, 179, italics in original.

23. Willard, *Spirit of the Disciplines*, 179.

24. Willard, *Spirit of the Disciplines*, 185.

25. See Michael Wear, *Reclaiming Hope: Lessons Learned in the Obama White House about the Future of Faith in America* (Nashville: Nelson, 2017), 229–39.

26. See Elisabeth Bumiller, "McCain Draws Line on Attacks as Crowds Cry 'Fight Back,'" *New York Times*, October 10, 2008, www.nytimes.com/2008/10/11/us/politics/11campaign.html.

27. Willard, *Spirit of the Disciplines*, 157–58.

28. In all this, you may even find yourself praying without what can sometimes be felt as the heavy burden of "prayer time."

Chapter 8: To Parents and Pastors

1. Dallas Willard, *Knowing Christ Today: Why We Can Trust Spiritual Knowledge* (San Francisco: HarperSanFrancisco, 2009), 193.

2. Willard, *Knowing Christ Today*, 197.

3. Willard, *Knowing Christ Today*, 198, italics in original.

4. Willard, *Knowing Christ Today*, 200.

5. Willard, *Knowing Christ Today*, 202.

6. Willard, *Knowing Christ Today*, 204.

7. Willard, *Knowing Christ Today*, 211.

8. Dallas Willard, foreword to *Spiritual Formation as If the Church Mattered*, by James C. Wilhoit (Grand Rapids: Baker Academic, 2008), xv, https://dwillard.org/articles/foreword-spiritual-formation -as-if-the-church-mattered.

9. Willard, *Knowing Christ Today*, 211.

10. Ryan Foley, "Many Pastors Say Christians Are More Loyal to Their Political Party Than to the Faith: Survey," *Christian Post*, November 20, 2022, www.christianpost.com/news/barna-pastors-cite -political-division-as-major-source-of-stress.html.

11. Willard, *Knowing Christ Today*, 196.

12. See Michael Wear, *Reclaiming Hope: Lessons Learned in the Obama White House about the Future of Faith in America* (Nashville: Nelson, 2018), 240.

13. Cited in Charles Homans and Alyce McFadden, "Today's Politics Divide Parties, and Friends and Families, Too," *New York Times*, October 18, 2022, www.nytimes.com/2022/10/18/us/politics/political -division-friends-family.html.

14. Cited in Samuel J. Abrams, "Are American Families Really Being Torn Apart by Politics?" Institute for Family Studies, September 20, 2021, https://ifstudies.org/blog/are-american-families-really-being -torn-apart-by-politics.

Chapter 9: There Will Be a Difference

1. Robert Coles, *The Moral Life of Children* (New York: Atlantic Monthly Press, 1986).

2. See "Ruby Bridges," Biography, updated February 23, 2021, www.bio graphy.com/activists/ruby-bridges.

3. Coles, *Moral Life of Children*, 22.

4. Coles, *Moral Life of Children*, 22–23.

5. Coles, *Moral Life of Children*, 23.

6. Coles, *Moral Life of Children*, 23–24.

7. Coles, *Moral Life of Children*, 24.

8. Coles, *Moral Life of Children*, 24.

9. Coles, *Moral Life of Children*, 25, italics in original.

10. See Valerie Strauss, "The Fate of Ruby Bridges's Historic School in New Orleans," *Washington Post*, November 28, 2020, www.washington post.com/education/2020/11/28/fate-ruby-bridgess-historic-school -new-orleans.

11. Dallas Willard, *Living in Christ's Presence: Final Words on Heaven and the Kingdom of God* (Downers Grove, IL: InterVarsity, 2014), 25.

12. Willard, *Living in Christ's Presence*, 25–26.

13. See "The United States President's Emergency Plan for AIDS Relief," U.S. Department of State, www.state.gov/pepfar, accessed June 1, 2023.

14. Dallas Willard, *Hearing God: Developing a Conversational Relationship with God* (Downers Grove, IL: InterVarsity, 2021), 10.

15. Dallas Willard, *The Divine Conspiracy: Rediscovering Our Hidden Life in God* (San Francisco: HarperSanFrancisco, 1998), 380.

16. Dallas Willard, *The Spirit of the Disciplines: Understanding How God Changes Lives* (San Francisco: HarperSanFrancisco, 1988), xii.

17. Willard, *Divine Conspiracy*, 21.

18. Willard, *Divine Conspiracy*, 385–86.

the Center for Christianity & Public Life

The Center for Christianity and Public Life (CCPL) is a nonpartisan nonprofit based in Washington, D.C., with the mission to contend for the credibility of Christian resources in public life, *for the public good.* The organization was founded by Michael Wear in 2022.

CCPL advances its mission through two streams of work: Christian Civic Formation and Public Imagination. The organization is grounded in the conviction that the kind of people we are has much to do with the kind of politics and public life that we have. Therefore, spiritual formation is central to civic renewal. In a frantic, anxious public square, CCPL offers a model of joyful confidence in Jesus, which opens up possibilities for a more gentle, just, and other-centered politics and culture.

If you would like to support the ideas in this book, consider supporting CCPL's work and mission. You can learn more about the Center for Christianity and Public Life at www.ccpubliclife.org.

We would be honored to join you in the life of faithfulness to which you have been called, to be faithful in all things, including public life.

From the Publisher

GREAT BOOKS

ARE EVEN BETTER WHEN THEY'RE SHARED!

Help other readers find this one:

- Post a review at your favorite online bookseller

- Post a picture on a social media account and share why you enjoyed it

- Send a note to a friend who would also love it—or better yet, give them a copy

Thanks for reading!